A HUNDRED THOUSAND WHITE STONES

A MEMOIR

Kunsang Dolma

with Evan Denno

WISDOM PUBLICATIONS · BOSTON

Wisdom Publications, Inc.
199 Elm Street
Somerville, MA 02144 USA
wisdompubs.org

Library of Congress Cataloging-in-Publication Data
Kunsang Dolma, 1980–
  A hundred thousand white stones : a memoir / Kunsang Dolma with Evan Denno.
    pages cm
  ISBN 978-1-61429-071-1 (paperback : alkaline paper) — ISBN 1-61429-071-7 (paperback : alkaline paper) — ISBN 978-1-61429-090-2 (ebook) (print)
  1. Kunsang Dolma, 1980– 2. Kunsang Dolma, 1980– Family. 3. Tibetan Americans—Biography. 4. Refugees—Biography. 5. Refugees—Family relationships—United States. 6. Refugees—Family relationships—China—Tibet Autonomous Region. 7. Intercountry marriage—United States. 8. Buddhist nuns—China—Tibet Autonomous Region—Biography. 9. Tibet Autonomous Region (China)—Biography. I. Denno, Evan. II. Title.
  E184.T53K86 2013
  951'.5—dc23

                                    2012045885

ISBN 978-1-61429-071-1
eBook ISBN 978-1-61429-090-2

17 16 15 14 13
5 4 3 2 1

Photographs courtesy of the author. Cover and interior design by Gopa&Ted2. Set in Nofrent 9.8/16. Cover photo of river bed by Shawn Rodriguez.

Wisdom Publications' books are printed on acid-free paper and meet the guidelines for permanence and durability of the Production Guidelines for Book Longevity of the Council on Library Resources.

Printed in the United States of America.

  This book was produced with environmental mindfulness. We have elected to print this title on 30% PCW recycled paper. As a result, we have saved the following resources: 11 trees, 6 million BTUs of energy, 983 lbs. of greenhouse gases, 5,331 gallons of water, and 357 lbs. of solid waste. For more information, please visit our website, www.wisdompubs .org. This paper is also FSC® certified. For more information, please visit www.fscus.org.

A HUNDRED THOUSAND WHITE STONES

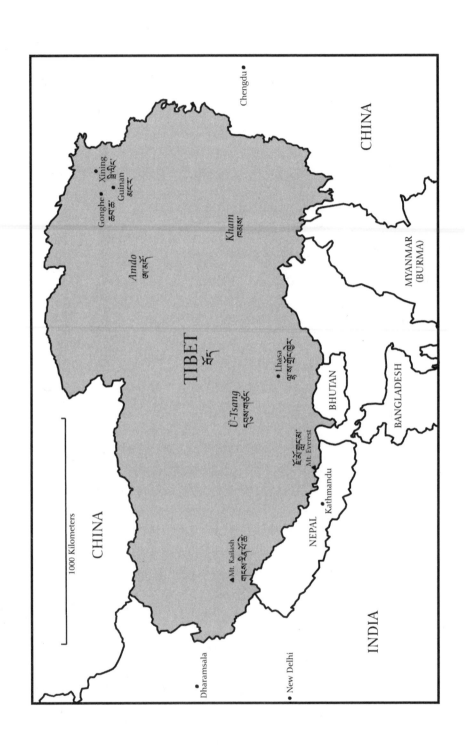

Contents

Introduction

L IKE MOST OF Tibet's refugees, I am neither a politician nor a saint; I am much like people from anywhere else in the world except for the experiences I've been through. I want to share my story because I don't know of any ordinary Tibetans like me who have spoken up about what we've seen and what's in our hearts. The process of going back through my history to write this book has not been easy. Some parts have been painful for me to revisit; many of the events in this book are ones I wish I could simply forget. For most of my life, I was ashamed of some of these experiences and told no one about them, not even my family or closest friends.

I was born in 1980 in a quiet village in the Amdo region of Tibet, where I lived until becoming a Buddhist nun as a teenager, a decision that led me to make the long and dangerous journey over the Himalayan Mountains into India to see the Dalai Lama. Although I gave up my nun's robes there under unfavorable circumstances, I did meet a good man, now my husband, leading to a family and new life in America.

The life I grew up with in Tibet was very simple. When I say "simple," I mean that we had what many people would consider a low standard of living, a life of poverty. I was born in a place without electricity or plumbing, with no cars, no telephones, and no television. Transportation was on foot or horseback. People knew almost nothing about the world outside of their own village and a few villages beyond it.

Even today, little has changed. Electricity was introduced to my village when I was around eleven or twelve years old. (Clocks and calendars were not widely used, so I'll have to guess my age and the dates of most of the events of my childhood.) When I was able to go back to Tibet in 2010, the use of electricity remained very limited, and there was still no plumbing. I saw that my family members do have clocks and calendars now. I'm not sure how much use they get though; the calendars have yellowed with age over the years since they were put up, and the clocks are motionless, each house stuck at a different time.

As a child, I didn't think our way of life in Tibet was any good at all. We worked hard with little to show for it, and our problems were deep, serious problems. Compared to the difficulties of daily life in Tibet, when Americans complain about a rough day, I can't help but think, "You've got to be kidding me!"

As I get older, I've come to see things a little differently than I did as a child. Leaving Tibet was not the end of my struggles in life; the struggles only changed. Although I know firsthand that Tibet is not a utopia and never was, people in my village were mostly pretty happy despite our circumstances. My favorite part of the traditional way of life was the close connection between family and friends. No matter what happened or how much we argued, we felt close. We lived and worked together, sharing our fortunes. Looking back on all my experiences, it seems like that feeling of personal connection with others is the real key to happiness. I wish now that I could have back the life I left behind.

1. The Invasion

BEGINNING IN 1949, the mountains and magic protecting Tibet were conquered by the technology and will of the Chinese Red Army. It isn't true that Tibetans never resisted this invasion violently. Before Dharma teachings from India reached Tibet, the people were once fierce warriors similar to the Mongolian horde. When our land was invaded, the fire in Tibetan hearts was still too strong to be held back by the peaceful influence of Buddhist teachings. Many people resisted as best they could with whatever weapons they had. Unfortunately for us, loosely organized farmers and shepherds with simple weapons were no match for a modern army. Resistance was virtually suicidal and ultimately a failure.

Life during the early years of occupation was little different than slavery. Villagers were forced to work for the Red Army without pay, and the soldiers could brutally beat them for any reason, or no reason at all. Hunger was the most serious problem. Prohibited from cooking on their own, villagers were forced to eat only at the single collective kitchen put in place by the soldiers. The kitchen served just one item, a thin soup made with a little flour mixed into a lot of water. When my parents looked at the soup, all they saw was the water. They always looked for meat and vegetables, but there never were any.

The villagers ate this soup for each meal every day for years. By the time circumstances improved enough for the villagers to get better food, their throats had become so weak from only drinking this thin soup that it was painful to swallow anything else. Even small pieces of bread softened in tea had become difficult to eat.

My mother worked in the kitchen in her village, where one of her jobs was serving the soup line. Each person was allowed exactly one ladleful of the soup for each meal. Forced to perform difficult physical labor while receiving such meager portions, everyone in the village was desperate to get as much soup as possible out of that one scoop of the ladle. Every single drop was a big deal to them. The extra time my mother took to let every drop from the ladle fall into each person's bowl has not been forgotten. During my youth many years later, I witnessed village elders express their passionate gratitude toward my mother for waiting for the drops to fall into their bowls.

Some other villagers assigned to the kitchen preferred to keep the line moving. After pouring the soup into each bowl, they pulled back the ladle right away, letting the extra drops fall back into the pot. That hasn't been forgotten either. Complaining about someone who didn't give them the extra drops was a common topic of conversation among elders during my childhood. As a child, unable to understand the suffering that these elders had lived through, I thought it was ridiculous to hear them talking so much about drops of soup.

My parents have told me that they often felt like dying right there where they sat after finishing their own bowls of soup. They were still so hungry when the soup was gone that they wished they could just give up. They felt as though there was no way they could get back up off the ground. Motivation was provided by the soldiers, who beat them until they started working again.

Many people died during this time. Some entire families died off. When the last member of a household died, it was known as "closing the gate." Every house in the village had a wall around the property with a gate in front. These gates were left open during the daytime to allow family members and visitors to come and go and locked closed at night. "Closing the gate" meant leaving a gate closed permanently. The village's closed gates stood out, silently reminding survivors of their lost friends and neighbors.

Neither of my grandfathers survived the occupation, and my father's mother died as well not long after the soldiers left her village. My father was still a teenager at this time and lived at home with his parents, doing his best to help them. He once managed to steal some flour and a few potatoes, which he tried to cook for his parents during the night. Although soldiers had taken away the pots and pans, my father could still prepare the potatoes in traditional Tibetan style nestled in the embers of the fire (the result is like a baked potato covered in ash). Smoke rose from the chimney as my father prepared the food. He didn't suspect the smoke would be a problem that late at night. It turned out the Chinese soldiers were watching after all; they did see the smoke and came to the house to grab my father.

Soldiers tied him up out in the sun the next day in a forced standing position, placed where everyone could see. He received no food or water all that day. Painful as the experience was, it wasn't enough to prevent him from trying again. He tried to steal food for them a few more times and always ended up getting caught and punished. Sometimes he was made to stand for long periods; other times he had to kneel on two overturned bowls while holding his arms up in the air. His body never fully recovered from the abuse, which has left him with lifelong pain. My father is a very flawed man, but I respect that he went to such great lengths to try to save his parents.

Working in her village kitchen gave my mother better opportunities for food theft. She prepared food for the soldiers as well as the villagers, and she once managed to steal a small chunk of the soldiers' meat. Her plan to give the meat to her mother ran into one problem: Her mother did not come home until very late that night. The chunk of meat had to wait out on the counter until she came home. Expecting that their mother would share part of the meat with her, my mother's sister was very excited to see it. While they waited for their mother to come home, my mother and her sister were tormented with hunger looking at this piece of meat that they were determined to save for her. They eventually went to bed before their mother returned, with the meat still on the counter. A cat soon saw its chance and jumped up on the counter to snatch it. The cat was too fast to catch and escaped beyond their reach, where it noisily chewed on the meat. Lying in bed in the darkness, my mother and her sister could hear every bite, knowing they would not be able to get the meat back from the cat. They both still think about that sound sometimes.

One of the best tricks local people used to steal food was to sew long thin bags to the inside of their pants. The idea was to slip barley grains into the bag a few at a time while working out in the fields. Villagers had to rub the barley between their hands and slip the individual grains into their bag without the soldiers, who watched them constantly, noticing what they were doing. If successful, they could chew on the raw grains later. If they were caught, they were beaten.

My mother's sister was very good at this trick, but my mother was not. Her sister often complained that she should have been trying harder to bring grain home for the family, but my mother was too scared and too tired to sneak many grains into her pouch. It was already so hard just keeping up with the work demanded by the soldiers that she didn't always have the energy to attempt this stressful and complicated practice. She succeeded only once. My mother's sister was steadily filling her bag that day while my mother held onto a few grains tucked in the palm of her hand. When the soldier watching them searched and caught her sister, my mother was able to quickly throw her little bit into her mouth.

The houses in this recent photo of my village are still built mainly by the families living in them. Families grow the trees seen in the background to use for future building projects.

Not all Chinese people are like these soldiers. There are ethnic Chinese farmers in some villages, and everyone has been getting along fine for as long as anyone can remember. The soldiers typically came from parts of China far away from Tibet. They weren't happy to be there, and they didn't respect the local people. Although most men in the village knew some Chinese language, these soldiers weren't very interested in communication. The soldiers just told people they were in charge and that everybody else had to shut up and get to work.

The Chinese soldiers were very proud of themselves for some reason. They seemed to have thought that they were very important people doing a very important job, but they didn't know anything about compassion. During the first few years of Chinese occupation, the soldiers were watching over a lot of people dying from hunger and severely beat these same people. Chinese soldiers today aren't much better. They still beat Tibetan people who are suffering under the occupation. It's hard to understand how one person could be so cruel to another. The cruelest insult heaped on these abuses during my parents' youth was that the villagers were regularly forced to sing patriotic Chinese songs in praise of the government in the midst of so much starvation and suffering.

The soldiers were allowed to steal anything they wanted. Most families in the village owned jewelry for weddings, typically coral necklaces, and tried to keep their jewelry safe from the soldiers by burying everything somewhere it wasn't likely to be found. Many of those secret locations were known to only one person and when that person died were lost forever. Even survivors sometimes forgot the exact place they buried their belongings. My mother's mother was one of the lucky few who both survived and found her jewelry again.

After the first few years of the occupation passed, the situation under Chinese control slowly improved. The soldiers started to leave, and people got the use of their land back, ending the time of starvation. It's not as though the occupation of Tibet turned out fine in the end, but it did get better. For me, when I look at what is happening in Tibet right now, I am angry and frustrated. For my parents, no matter what the Chinese government does now, they're always glad that at least the current situation is an improvement over the days of hunger.

2. My Parents

M Y PARENTS WERE teenagers when the soldiers left their villages and life started to improve. They married not long after life in the area settled down. Their relationship wasn't exactly a love story. Marriages are arranged in Tibetan culture, and as is customary, they were from different villages. It's unlikely my parents had ever met before their wedding day.

Tibetan marriage arrangements usually start with the grandparents knowing each other or the parents getting information from a friend. What parents are looking for is someone from a family that is stable, honest, and competent at farm skills. Because either the bride or groom (most often the bride) has to move in with the other family, the personality of the whole family is important. When Tibetan marriages run into problems, it's more often the result of conflict between the in-laws and the new family member than between the husband and wife.

Americans who hear about arranged marriages may tend to think they're a bad idea. From what I've seen, though, arranged marriages can actually work out well. The Tibetan tradition is that it isn't okay to have a boyfriend or girlfriend before marriage, and divorce is uncommon. Occasionally a young man and young women express an interest in each other, and their parents take that into consideration.

When parents decide on a marriage, their son or daughter has to give love to the person the parents choose. Everybody has the same expectations, and they usually do have a good relationship.

Weddings are very special in Tibet. Everyone watching can imagine how nervous the new husband and wife must be, especially the one moving in with a new family in a new village. There's no government document or religious authority at the wedding, just a social agreement and a party. The party starts early in the morning and lasts late into the night, with everyone of all ages coming together for food, singing, and conversation. It's always a very comfortable, relaxed occasion. There's no set schedule to follow; even the bride and groom show up whenever they're ready. The families of the bride and groom wear their fanciest chubas, the traditional Tibetan garment; everyone else can come as they are.

My parents didn't have much money or much of anything at all after their marriage. They survived by growing what they needed for food and eventually saved up enough money to buy some sheep and cows and later horses. They stayed in my father's village, Maktangcun, until his mother died, then moved to my mother's village to be closer to family. My mother had a brother and two sisters in her village. Family support can be critical in Tibetan life, since families typically share labor and help each other during hard times.

Like everyone else in the area, my parents struggled to recover from the loss of family livestock during the invasion. Animals were families' main wealth, essentially their life savings. Before the invasion, most families in my area owned milking cows, workhorses, pigs, chickens, and sheep or goats. Sheep or goats were typically a family's most important possession. Tending to flocks for food, trade, and sale was the core of the village economy.

As part of their effort to rebuild, the people in my mother's village pooled all the money they had managed to hide from the soldiers to buy some sheep and goats for the village to collectively share. My father worked for the village watching all the sheep. In exchange he was given some meat and a little money.

The village also practiced collective agriculture at that time. Collective agriculture was a stupid idea, and it was an especially bad deal for my family. The village assigned points for each member of a family who worked on the collective farm on a given day and deducted points based on total members of the family. If a family had extra points at the end of the year, they received money; families with negative points had to pay a penalty. The problem for my parents was that points were deducted for each family member without consideration of age. Only my mother and oldest brother were working on the farm at the time. My father was busy with the sheep, and the other kids were too young to work. At the end of the year, my family would owe the village money they didn't have.

My parents always had just enough to feed the family with almost nothing left over. The only time they had a chance to relax and enjoy life was on Losar, the Tibetan New Year. Losar is the one time of year when poor farmers spend money on luxuries like meat and alcohol. My father was working very hard for the family at that point in his life, and this was the one time of year he got to take it easy with something to drink. The family didn't have money, but on Losar everybody got a chance to drink and enjoy life whether they had money or not.

One year my mother had absolutely no money at all to celebrate Losar. She knew that my father was seriously looking forward to his big chance to have a drink, so she went to visit her brother and sisters to ask for money to buy whiskey. Whiskey was very cheap then, maybe the equivalent of about a few cents. None of them gave her anything. Although she was a proud person, she asked everybody she could think of to lend her enough money to buy at least a little whiskey. In the end, she got no money to buy the whiskey for my father.

That year, on the first night of Losar, my father came home from watching the sheep certain he was going to get some whiskey. He was surprised that my mother poured him tea when he got home. He waited and didn't say anything. He could tell my mother was not happy, that she was only pretending to smile for Losar. After dinner, he was still waiting. He waited for a long time, and he didn't say anything and my mother didn't say anything. Finally he asked her where the whiskey was. My mother started to cry as she told my father that she wasn't able to get any money. He got angry when he heard that and scolded her for not asking her brother or sisters. He couldn't believe they hadn't lent anything.

They were both disappointed and hurt that my mother's family wouldn't help them. There's a Tibetan saying: "If you're rich, your name is Sir, and if you're poor, your name is Hey Ugly." It looked as if my mother's brother and sisters thought that way, like they didn't want to take care of a poor family that couldn't return the favor later.

After that, my father told my mother it was time for them to move back to his village. In my mother's village, they had to listen to my mother's family sharing their unwelcome opinions about what my parents should be doing. He thought it was better not to be around family if they weren't going to help anyway. I think my father just wanted to get away from where they were.

The move back to my father's village is one of the few events I do know the date for. It was 1980. My mother was eight months pregnant, and I was about to enter the story. My mother must have had a very tough time walking the considerable distance to my father's village with a baby on the way. I've been pregnant, and I can't imagine it. To add to the challenge, there was trouble from Zondija and Prri, my twin older brothers. They were very small, traveling in baskets on the back of a horse-drawn cart. They were trying to reach each other and fight the whole way. A few times, they almost got out of their baskets.

I am the youngest of the eight kids in my family. Though my parents were only fifteen when they were first married, they didn't have any children until they were twenty-eight. All those years they had been waiting and hoping, and still no babies. At that time, there was no birth control, so after thirteen years without a child, it looked like they definitely weren't going to be able to have any children, which are essential to help with the work on a farm. My father's sister already had two kids and felt sorry for my parents' situation, so when she was pregnant a third time she told my father, "Look, this is my third child. I'm going to give him to you." The baby was twenty-two days old when my parents took him home. After that, my mother started to have her own babies. My parents always thought that my adopted brother Yula had brought them good luck.

There's a story behind my family's bad luck until then. The bad luck was my father's brother's fault. This uncle had a classic cowboy personality. He was uneducated but clever, rough but handsome, and a manly tough guy. He would go out on horseback for days at a time, up to his own mysterious business. Women loved him, and he loved women back, but he was not a family man. When he got a woman pregnant, he didn't stick around. An angry father brought a curse on my uncle and his whole family. That was the reason my parents couldn't have children for so many years.

This father was a follower of the Nyingma school of Buddhism. Of the major branches of Buddhism in Tibet, the Nyingma school is the oldest, and it is the school that retains the most of Tibet's pre-Buddhist religious culture. Before Buddhism reached Tibet, religious culture focused on nature spirits and included practices similar to magic. So it was presumed that the father of this woman knew some kind of magic and had cursed my uncle. Soon after abandoning the daughter, my uncle dropped dead. One day he was strong and healthy, and then the next day he died. I don't have any proof to show he was killed by a curse, but that's what happened.

My parents standing in fields in front of the village chorten.
My mother is wearing a chuba and carrying a traditional
basket used for farm work.

The situation for the rest of the family soon got worse too. Any time
my family saved a little money, an unexpected expense would come
up that quickly took that money away. My father's description of the
situation was that it was like having a bucket of water with a leak on
the bottom. Nothing they put in the bucket stayed very long. My father

asked a lama how to fix the problem and was told there was nothing for him to do. He would have to wait for the curse to slowly wear off.

One effect of this curse was that my family's horses disappeared. New foals were born every year, but the number of horses owned by my family always got smaller. The last of the horses was a prized white horse that was famous in the village for its beauty and hard work. When that horse went missing too, my father looked for it in every nearby village without any luck. Work and travel were both much more difficult without any horses. For our family, losing the last horse was like a person losing his or her right hand. My father eventually had to give up searching and gather what money the family had to buy a new horse.

My father went to the closest city with the money. My family thinks the curse made him go there, because anyone, even a child, would know they should buy horses in the village. Not long after he arrived in the city, my father was grabbed by the neck from behind and thrown to the ground. He woke up with a bruise across his throat and without his money. The police didn't even want to listen to his story.

Yula, whose addition to the family started the gradual end of this curse, is about twenty-two years older than I am. After they adopted Yula, my parents had five more boys, including twins, and my sister. Most of my siblings had grown up enough to be doing work on the farm by the time I was born. As they grew up and took over the family's responsibilities, my father began doing less and less of the work himself and drinking more.

My father was a complete alcoholic by the time I was born. In our village, he could drink almost every day even without much money of his own. Whenever any of the alcoholics in the village got his hands on any money, he bought whiskey and then gathered all the other alcoholics to get drunk together. Sometimes they went to one of their houses; other times they spent the day in the shade of a tree passing a bottle. Although my father was rarely the person buying the whiskey, everybody in the village had known each other for a long time, so they always shared with him.

My father's alcoholism put my mother in a difficult situation during her pregnancy with me. She had to take care of the family mostly on her own, and pregnancy in Tibet was already difficult in the best circumstances. My mother never went to a hospital or saw a doctor when she gave birth to any of her kids. Women in the village usually called over neighbors or family who lived nearby when they started going into labor. My mother had nobody. She was alone for the births of all of her children except the twins. She even cut her own umbilical cords.

For the birth of the twins, my father's sister was with my mother. They didn't know she was carrying twins until she gave birth to them. My mother thought she was done after just one twin, then another baby came, and my father's sister thought there might be a third. When my father's sister told her a third baby was coming, my mother yelled out, "God help me. If there are three of them, it's better if you kill me."

While pregnant with me, my mother already had her hands full with the kids she already had and didn't want any more. She also had to think about the kind of life another baby was going to have, given my father's alcoholism and the extreme poverty of the family. I don't know what my father thought about the pregnancy one way or another; he was drinking so much by then he didn't really care what was going on anymore.

My mother decided to end the pregnancy. She didn't have any-where she could go for an abortion, so she tried to induce a miscar-riage on her own. The work on Tibetan farms is hard manual labor, and any time my mother had boxes to carry, large rocks to move, or anything like that, she put all these things on her stomach through-out the day. Fortunately for me, it didn't work. I believe my mother was also glad that she failed to lose the baby. She has told me that she felt lucky that the baby didn't die because now she has me.

3. Fresh-Air Childhood

IT WAS NECESSARY for an adult to watch kids in the village until they could walk. After that, they could start going out with older kids. In most families, there were older siblings, cousins, or friends' kids who could go out with the younger ones. Nobody thought it was dangerous to give children this much freedom, and I can't think of any situations where it turned out badly. It helped that there were no cars to worry about, mostly just some cows and horses.

Kids usually spent the day outside together in groups. When the kids in one of the groups got hungry, they could go into any of their homes to get food and go right back outside when they finished eating. If kids got tired, they might go home to sleep, or they might lie down and take a nap in the grass any place they were comfortable. It was a pretty wild childhood, and I loved it.

I usually went out with the neighbors' kids. My older siblings were busy working on the farm, and the twins, who were the closest to me in age, were too wild to take care of me. The twins went off by themselves, and if they saw me they always gave me a hard time, like throwing rocks in my direction. My neighbor had two girls around my age I played with, often making something we thought looked like baby dolls with our jackets. All the kids in the village played together a lot of the time, too, using whatever objects we found around the village for our toys.

One of my favorite games when I got a little older was inspired by Chinese war movies that were sometimes shown in the village during the winter. The movies portrayed the Red Army fighting invading Japanese soldiers. In the movies, the Chinese soldiers were great heroes. They were kind, brave, and triumphant in every encounter with the Japanese. As a kid, I didn't know any better and thought the Chinese soldiers were great. I even wanted to be a soldier too when I grew up. We copied the movies by using jawbones from pigs or goats as guns. There would be a group of kids who were supposed to be the Japanese and another group who were the Chinese, all running around the village pretending to shoot each other.

When I was about eight years old, I was responsible for babysitting for my mother's friend from another village. Grandparents typically took care of their grandchildren while the parents were out working, but this friend of my mother didn't have family around, and there were no daycares or babysitters to hire. I'm not sure quite how old her son was. He must have been very young because he couldn't crawl yet when I started to take care of him.

The hardest part was taking the baby out to nurse with his mother, who was working in the fields. I wish I'd had a back carrier then like the one I later had for my daughters in America. Instead of a back carrier, I had to wrap a piece of fabric around the baby and tie him in front of me to stabilize him on my back. It was a long walk to bring the baby to his mother like that. I would walk and walk, fall down, and then have to tie the baby back on again because the fabric would come undone. This particular little boy was extra big and heavy. His father was the tallest and biggest person ever in the village. Everybody called him Big Guy. When I came back to visit Tibet many years later, I wasn't surprised to see that the baby had grown up to be every bit as big as his father.

The sun was very hot all that summer, and I didn't have any umbrella or sun hat to protect me. I would be dripping with sweat as

I carried him. After I got him out to his mother and he was finished nursing, I had to do it all again on the way back. I also had to clean up his poop, get him to nap, and feed him. There were no diapers in those days, just a square hole in the back of his pants. I had to clean his bottom with the smooth stones scattered around on the ground. This went on for four or five months, an entire summer.

I was jealous of the other kids my age playing or doing what they wanted without any worries or responsibility. I hated that I couldn't go out with my friends. They looked so happy playing and laughing with each other. I was only eight years old and felt like a mother to this boy. For most of my life after that, I was sure I never wanted to have kids myself.

4. A Blessing from the Panchen Lama

AROUND THAT SAME AGE, I had the good fortune to see the Panchen Lama, Tibet's second most important spiritual teacher. He was traveling throughout Tibet and made a stop not very far from my village. It was an amazing opportunity for the poor villagers from my area. I don't remember any teaching or ceremony taking place at the time. He was getting old; it looked like he came only to make sure people had a chance to see him before he died.

The event was in Gonghe, too far away for my whole family to go. We couldn't travel that far on our tractor, and my family didn't have money to pay for everyone to get a ride on one of the commercial trucks being used to carry villagers to the city. My family could afford for five of us to go: my parents, my older brothers, and me. My other five siblings stayed home. My parents and older brothers had the benefit of seniority, and I got to go because I was the youngest.

We stayed with a cousin who lived in Gonghe. In addition to us, a crowd of other extended family members had come from all over to stay with the cousin, far too many people to fit in the house. My family had to sleep in a tent the cousin set up in his yard. Sleeping outside didn't bother us, and we appreciated that the cousin and his family treated everyone very well. The cousin had a car he took us around in, which was new and very exciting to me. When I got back home from seeing the Panchen Lama, I mostly talked about riding in the car.

As the audience to see the Panchen Lama involved too many people to fit inside any spaces within the city, the event was held outside the city, in a large empty space, the kind of flat grassy expanse common in Tibet. He sat in a chair, blessing the people who came before him by placing his hand on top of each person's head. Older people, including my parents, received small photos of the Panchen Lama from the monks attending to him.

The crowd was massive and packed closely together. My father had to carry me on his shoulders any time we were inside the crowd to make sure I didn't get lost or crushed. To accommodate this huge group of people, the blessings went on all day for four or five days. At his age, there was no way for the Panchen Lama to put his hand on that many heads without help. Monks had to help hold up his hand and put it down on people's heads as they came up to him.

On the second day of blessings, the Panchen Lama addressed the crowd over a microphone, asking everyone to wait patiently and not push. He told the crowd that children and old people could get hurt if everyone pushed to get to the front, and said not to worry—if people waited patiently, he would get to everyone. Despite what he said, people continued to push. Talk within the crowd encouraged fears he might get sick or exhausted and have to leave before finishing all the blessings.

After receiving their blessings, people left to make room for the others. Even so, it took time for the crowd to shrink. My family had to come for several days before we could get through. Early one of those mornings, we were lucky enough to have the chance to be part of a line of people waiting along the road for the Panchen Lama to pass by. He rode by us in the open bed of a truck, waving to everyone. Later, after days of trying, we did eventually receive our blessings.

I feel very fortunate I had the opportunity to receive this important blessing. The current incarnation of the Panchen Lama has been unable to provide us with teachings and blessings, since he is being held in captivity by the Chinese government without contact with the Tibetan people. I hope that he is safe and will be able to communicate with us during my lifetime.

5. A Little Education

WHERE I LIVED, kids weren't required to go to school, and many didn't. Most kids from my village were either too busy with farm work or just weren't interested. I'd guess that maybe 30 to 40 percent of the kids in the village attended school at some point in their lives. None of my siblings did. As the youngest in my family, I grew up at a time when my brothers and sister had the farm work under control, making it possible for my family to pay the small fee for school as well as the expense of books, which would have otherwise been hard to pay. I was the only one of us to receive any education.

I started school when I was around eleven years old. I wanted to attend school because I thought education could lead to a government job one day. If I had a government job, I knew my family would always have enough money. In school we learned math, Chinese language, and the Tibetan alphabet. Our studies were based entirely on repetition and memorization. For example, to teach the Chinese alphabet, the teacher gave us specific sentences to memorize. After we learned the alphabet, we were given stories to memorize. For the big exam at the end of the year we were expected to write out an entire story perfectly.

At the start of class in the morning, the teacher picked one of us to write the homework on the blackboard. I had to study constantly at home to prepare for the days I was picked, leaving no time to play or help my mother. The price for mistakes was no joke. If a student didn't get everything perfectly right, the teacher would get out his ruler. Holding up the ruler, he asked how many times that student wanted to get hit on the palm of his or her hand. Everybody would rather be hit zero times if we really had a choice, but we would only end up getting hit more if we asked for a small number. If we asked for just one or two hits we would get ten or twenty for sure. The teacher hit absolutely as hard as he could. My hand turned completely red whenever I was hit; it felt like being cut with a knife.

A few other students and I were once given a special punishment for our mistakes on a small exam. To inspire us to try harder next time, the teacher had us stand on top of the wall around the school starting early in the morning. He didn't tell us when we could come down. We stayed there through lunch, through the afternoon, and were still there when the sun was going down after all the other students had gone home. My mother and sister-in-law saw us from out in the field. Her own eyes too weak to see us clearly, my mother asked my sister-in-law every few minutes if we had come down yet. We stayed for as long as we did because students in my class normally never went home until the teacher told us to, and we were afraid of making the teacher angry. Eventually we saw the teacher go into a small shop across the river. The teacher lived at the school but had obviously left without saying anything to us. When we saw that, we finally came down. One of the boys couldn't walk. He had to be carried home by two other boys holding him from each side.

Any student who didn't score better than 60 percent on the end-of-the-year exams had to leave school. Failing the exams typically left students with no choice other than to return to their family farms. Students who made it to high school or college before failing out of school had a difficult time finding a husband or wife when they came back to the village. Villagers believed that people who hadn't grown up doing farm work as children wouldn't be able to handle all the work as adults and would probably screw it up anyway. No one wanted to arrange a marriage with someone like that.

We sometimes saw the teacher around the village when we were out on the weekends. Even though there was no class and we weren't doing anything wrong, we would flee from him as fast as we could. I don't think the teacher enjoyed us students very much either, and he avoided us too, including when he was supposed to be teaching us. Once a person got a government job, including teaching, there was no way to get fired. Any time the teacher had somewhere else he'd rather be, he told us, "I've got to go; you guys be good," and nobody had a problem with it. Sometimes the teacher never showed up for class at all.

We were never good when that happened. We usually spent the day fighting until it was time to go home. I don't remember ever fighting with other kids before I started school. As a student, I fought all the time. There weren't many other girls in the class, so I usually had to fight with boys. My head still has a number of small scars from being hit with rocks while I was a student. When I was a nun and shaved my head, everyone could see these scars and knew I was a lot of trouble as a kid.

My time in school also left me with two tattoos. I made them on my left hand using a jar of ink, a sewing needle, and a stick on days the teacher didn't come. First I dipped the stick into the jar of ink and used it to draw the designs. Once the designs were laid on my hand with a thick coat of ink, I jabbed my skin with the sewing needle. To be sure the designs stayed, I had to push the needle all the way under my skin each time. Between the two tattoos it must have taken hundreds of jabs to complete the work. The first of the tattoos is a simple arrangement of six dots on the fleshy part between my thumb and index finger. The second is an *Om* on my wrist.

Despite the tattoos, scars, scratches, bruises, and hating everything about school, I didn't think about quitting; it meant a lot to me that I was the only one in my family with the opportunity to get a stable government job one day. It didn't work out though. I ended up staying in school for only two years, not nearly enough to work for the government. I had to give up going to school to help my mother with the cooking and cleaning for our large family. Attitudes are starting to change now, but the way it used to be was that there were jobs that were for men and jobs for women. No matter how many brothers I had, it was out of the question for them to do women's work, leaving it up to me to help my mother since my sister had moved away after her marriage. I didn't have another chance to continue my education until I escaped into India.

6. Life in the Village

AFTER DROPPING OUT of school, I went back to farm life alongside my family. Daily routines on the farm shifted with the seasons. Some times of year were absolutely backbreaking, while at other times there was almost no work to do. Our plants and animals set the schedule. It was a simple and peaceful way of life. I wish now that I had appreciated it more as a child. At the time, I only saw the hard work and wanted to get away from the farm. What I didn't recognize then was the togetherness of my family, our independence, and the peace that came from the simplicity of village life.

Families like mine with flocks of sheep or goats had to start the day early. Unless someone stayed out with the flock, the sheep and goats were kept in pens overnight, then taken out to pasture with the first light of the morning. A fire needed to be set and breakfast made before one of the family members (most often my father, and later the twins) went out with our flock. Beginning when I was around eleven years old, I was responsible for making that breakfast, feeding a large family with big appetites from constant physical labor. I hated getting up so early and frequently complained about it to my mother. She used to tell me that one day when we weren't so busy she would let me stay in bed and sleep all day. I really looked forward to that day, but it never came.

Wolves posed a serious threat to my family's flock of sheep. If a wolf gets the chance to attack an unprotected flock, it can be devastating. Wolves tend to kill many sheep or goats, eating only the best parts. When threatened by a wolf, the first instinct for sheep is to run. The problem is that the fastest sheep gets nervous that it can't see the rest of the flock, so it turns around to get back inside the group. The other sheep try to follow the leader, causing the whole flock to start running in a circle. The wolf can relax and wait for them to get tired.

Guard dogs in Tibet that protect the sheep from wolves at night are very different from pet dogs people keep in America. Tibetan guard dogs are supposed to be wild and dangerous. When I used to walk around my village, dogs were always barking and pulling at their chains as if they would eat me if they got the chance. When I first came to America, it was very strange for me to see dogs treated like part of the family. I wasn't sure bringing them inside the house was a good idea. Now that I've gotten used to it, though, I actually think that the care people have for their pets is one of the positive qualities of American culture. I've also noticed that Americans typically have smaller families and bigger houses than Tibetans do, so it makes sense to have pets around to make the space feel less empty.

Although I never had to take out the sheep myself, my jobs weren't much easier. Spring started out fairly quietly for me with the usual cooking and cleaning, then once the barley seeds sprouted, it was time to pull weeds. My mother and I still had to cook breakfast, and when that was done, we headed into the field. Women did most of the weeding because men tended to step all over the barley whenever they helped. My mother and I pulled weeds all day long with the hot sun over us. The next day, plenty of new weeds would be there, and we had to pull them all day long all over again. The only break was for lunch: bread and tea from a thermos. After weeding, there was dinner to make. My family ate quickly in the candlelight and went to bed soon after dark, completely exhausted.

Fall was especially busy for all of us for one month of bringing in the harvest; then once the harvest was in, life slowed down. With the exception of the person who still had to take out the sheep and goats, the rest of us had very little to do. When not busy most Tibetans love to slowly cook and slowly eat, especially my mother. Slowly cooking and slowly eating can easily fill the day. We'd start cooking breakfast when we got up, get lunch going by the time breakfast was over, then enjoy a tea break followed by dinner. After dinner was over and the cleanup done, it would be getting close to bedtime. My mother loved those days.

With no electricity, there was nothing to do but go to bed after dark. Unable to sleep so early on short winter days, we'd spend a long time awake in bed talking, occasionally getting up to find a snack. Two of my brothers and my sister were already married and had moved out. Among those of us still in the house, my four brothers shared a bed, and I slept with my parents. Our beds were made of packed dirt covered by blankets. The best part was a hollow space at the bottom we'd fill with hot ashes, keeping the bed warm through the night. In the winter, a dirt bed with hot ashes is by far the best way to sleep.

7. Tibetan Cooking

THE FOOD WE ATE was very simple with little variety. Nobody ever asked me if I wanted to eat this or eat that, or whether I liked the food I was given. Breakfast and lunch were almost always bread and tea. Occasionally there were fried vegetables or potato soup to go with it. Dinner was always exactly the same thing. In the dialect spoken in my village, the word for "dinner" and the word for the noodle soup we always ate for dinner are the same: thukpa. Thukpa is made with homemade noodles boiled in a soup flavored with garlic chives. There are several ways to make the noodles; the simplest way is to take strips of the dough and pull off small pieces flattened by your thumb as you tear them from the strip. I've eaten an incredible amount of thukpa over my lifetime, and it's still my favorite food.

In America, there are so many choices, and the food is a lot fancier. I can eat anything I want, but I don't enjoy food in America like I did in Tibet. For me the people sharing the meal are much more important than the food. If I am around family having a nice conversation, I feel happy no matter what we are eating. Even if the food is absolutely great, without good company eating just feels like a job. If I didn't have to eat to live, I would probably skip most meals unless I were in good company. I'm used to a big family and people always coming over to visit and eat together. In my experience—and I think this is true for most Tibetans—the more people are eating together, the better the food tastes.

When visiting a friend in Tibet, sharing food is an important part of the experience. People in my village always cook more food than their family is going to eat so they'll be ready when visitors come. If a friend comes by right when the family is finishing dinner, it's no problem; everyone is happy to start dinner all over again to give the friend some company. If a visitor comes when it's not close to a mealtime, there's always bread and tea. There is no way to leave a Tibetan house without at least having some bread and tea first. To avoid the appearance of visiting for the free food, the Tibetan habit when visiting friends is to pretend to be full already and in fact to have eaten too much. The host, in turn, insists that every visitor eats. No matter what visitors say, the host puts food in front of them, and if someone doesn't pick it up, the host shoves it into the guest's hand. Tibetans living in exile often find it confusing when their non-Tibetan friends take offense at this type of hospitality.

Most years the only time we ate meat was during Losar. It was our big chance. Every Losar I would eat as many meat momos (a Tibetan version of dumplings) as I could, and every year I got sick afterward. It was worth it. When I eat momos now, I still feel like I should eat as many of them as possible.

Although meat isn't often available, few Tibetans are practicing vegetarians. The Dalai Lama and other very good people don't eat meat, and the rest of us know that the best thing for Buddhists is that we don't either, but most regular people are happy to eat meat if they can get it. Tibetans think meat will make them strong, and people who work hard on the farm all day long are looking for that.

In Tibet there are no neat packages of butchered meat in a store; if someone is going to eat meat, the person sees the animal die and feels compassion for it. Tibetans prefer killing large animals so that many people can have food from taking only one animal's life. It's considered very bad to kill many small animals to make just one meal. It's bad for karma and people feel bad about each time they take a life. It's also considered better to kill an animal raised by humans than an animal that lives in the wild. I'm not exactly sure why that is, but I think it's because wild animals have freedom and are not dependent on human care. Eating anything that lives in the water is the worst. Although we have beautiful rivers filled with fish flowing through the area around my village, Tibetans never eat fish no matter how poor and hungry they are.

8. Losar

LOSAR IS A HIGHLIGHT of the year for most Tibetans. It's our only holiday, and it's a good one. During Losar the entire village celebrates for fifteen days. People can really relax over that amount of time. The only work that needs to be done is basic animal care.

Preparations for Losar begin ten days before the holiday starts. Plenty of momos are made, along with certain breads and other special foods. Every inch of the house, every bowl and piece of furniture, has to be cleaned from every angle. People also wash themselves as best they can before going to bed on the eve of Losar.

Adults get up right at midnight to greet the New Year with fireworks and prayers. Waking up the neighbors is not a problem; everybody is part of the celebration. Everyone prays, and smoke offerings are made to spiritual beings. By making smoke offerings, we hope to promote a positive relationship between the people in the village and the spiritual beings in the area that consume the smoke. If the spiritual beings are happy and appreciative, they have ways they can help people in return.

Around two in the morning, the kids in the village get up. The tradition for children on the first day of Losar is similar to Halloween. Children go around the village from house to house, knocking on doors to get candy. There are no costumes like Halloween, though all the children wear new clothes. Older people enjoy seeing the kids and commenting on their cute new clothes, and the kids like the candy.

Running around in the dark at that time of the night was always a challenge. Of course we fell down sometimes. When we'd fall, some of the candy usually fell out of our pockets, and we had to try to find it all again, which wasn't easy in the dark. I found the best way to make sure I got all the candy back was to remember where I fell and return when the sun came up.

After the sun comes up, the adults start going out to visit friends and family. Visiting goes on for several days. There's no rush to get to any particular house, and there's no central meal or event. People slowly go around the village to see everybody they want to talk to, making sure to spend some time with any and all extended family members.

Food is always ready over these first few days of Losar. Tibetans would be extremely embarrassed if anyone came to visit and there wasn't anything to eat. The food doesn't have to be fancy; there just has to be enough of it to feed everyone who comes by. Most of it is prepared ahead of time and kept in cold outdoor storage rooms so the women in the village aren't kept busy by cooking the whole time.

The main part of Losar occurs after the first few days of visits, when people from neighboring villages gather to compete in friendly contests of archery and singing. The number of villages participating changes every year; some years several villages get together, while other years just two villages compete. The location of the competition switches between the villages daily. Families from the different villages connect to take turns hosting each other at the end of the day.

I don't know very much about the archery; it's mostly something men enjoy. From what I've seen, the men competing all get two shots apiece at a target made of packed earth. The person that hits the closest to the middle of the target wins that round for his village, and then they start over again. It looks boring to me, but the men are passionate about these archery contests. Every time someone gets a good shot that hits closer to the center than any other shot so far, the men like to run around and yell about it.

After sunset the focus shifts from archery to singing. The singing isn't exactly a contest like the archery. It's mostly just for enjoyment, with a sense of pride involved in the performance of each village's singers. Men and women sing alternately in evolving narratives that are usually love-themed.

Improvisational skills are as important as a nice voice to make a great singer. The person singing holds a scarf (or a more decorative ceremonial scarf called a khatak, if they have one), which he or she can pass off to any one of the participants of the opposite gender. Whoever the singer chooses has to be able to pick up the thread of the song where the last person left off, specifically responding to the last person's comments while maintaining the overall flow of the song.

These love songs can be sweet and romantic, but they aren't always. The songs are often funny, teasing, or scolding. Singers sometimes give each other a very hard time. People's feelings are not easily hurt in Tibet, so singers can say just about anything without worrying that another person is going to be offended. In Tibet, if someone is fat or old or wears ugly clothes, it's fine to say so, and Losar singing is a good time to bring these things up.

It does sometimes happen that Losar love songs turn into some-thing more than just a song. Young men and women occasionally try to keep in touch after singing romantically to each other on Losar, and once in a while those relationships lead to marriage. Young men always seemed to prefer to pass the scarf to cute women, probably hoping that the song would turn into love.

Despite all the festivity, Losar was not always a happy time for me. It was the time of year I most strongly felt my family's poverty. Traditionally everybody buys new clothes to wear for the New Year celebrations. For my family, spending money on clothes for all the children was out of the question. I'm not a very fancy person, but as a girl I did want to look pretty once in a while, and I wanted to be like the other kids.

I loved going around the village on the first morning of Losar yelling "Happy Losar!" and getting candy, but my old clothes made me feel ashamed. I wore the same clothes every day until they were absolutely too old to keep using, well past the point of being worn out and showing a long history of stains. The best I could hope for on Losar would be old clothes handed down from my sister. Some years I had to wear the same clothes I wore every other day. The other kids wouldn't exactly tease me about it; they would look at me and then look back at each other and laugh together. I'm not stupid. I knew they were laughing at me.

To get the candy without being laughed at, I would make sure I saw other kids before they saw me. If I saw kids with nice new clothes on, I stayed away, and if I saw kids with clothes not much better than my own, I went over to play with them. There were some years I just stayed home. My mother knew what was going on, and it hurt her that she wasn't able to do better for us. The rest of the village looked forward to Losar, and my mother always hated it.

9. My Father's Drinking

WHILE MY MOTHER did her best to look after us, my alcoholic father mostly made things worse for the family. When I think back to memories of my mother from my childhood, I remember her being constantly busy for most of the year. She had the barley field to worry about; cows, horses, and pigs to feed; and on top of that she was taking care of the house and raising us kids. She always walked fast. If I ever stopped to play or complain when I was walking with her, she kept right on going. Meanwhile, as she was moving, almost running, from job to job, none of us were sure exactly where my father was most of the time.

More often than not, he was out drinking. We never knew when to expect him home, and when he did come home after drinking was the worst part. The more he drank, the more he became demanding, selfish, and violent. We were all afraid of him. He would beat any of us he found when he got home, usually my mother. He would beat her with a shovel or whatever else he got his hands on. One time he broke her nose with a bottle.

If we heard from a neighbor that my father was drunk and on the way home, we all had to eat quickly, then get out of the house before he got there. It was usually safe to come home later, after my father fell asleep. We used to go outside to hide for some time before coming back to check on him. My mother would peek into the house first, then slowly and quietly go inside. If my father were asleep, we could all quietly come in behind her and go to bed. The times it was getting late and he hadn't fallen asleep yet, we had to stay out for the night. My brothers usually spent the night sleeping in our haystack while my mother and I slept at a neighbor's house. Sometimes my father came looking for us.

He once found the house where my mother and I were hiding. He yelled and banged on the gate until my mother's friend got out of bed to open the gate for him. She lied, telling him that we weren't there and scolded him for making so much noise. He insisted on coming inside to look for us anyway. She was divorced and living alone, so she didn't try to stop him. From our hiding place under a chuba in a closet, I could see my father come in. He was very drunk and angry, very scary looking. He must have had a hard time finding warm clothes in the dark while this drunk, because he was wearing my sister's pink jacket. The jacket was much too tight for him, and the sleeves didn't quite reach his hands. We kept as quiet as possible, almost holding our breath until he left. That night I think he probably banged on every gate in the village trying to find us.

The scariest experience was the time my mother had already left before I got home. I was probably eight or nine at the time. I was home with the twins, Zondija and Prri, who were three years older than me. We were sleeping when my father came home, awoken suddenly by the sound of him yelling as he came through the gate. It was completely dark when he came in, and there was no electricity or flashlight to help us see what was going on. We dressed as fast as we could, looking around for our mother while putting on our clothes. My father banged on the door and yelled for us to let him in, but we were so scared of him, we definitely were not going to open up that door. We waited inside, not knowing what to do. My father grabbed a shovel and started hitting the door with it. Terrified, we tried to escape out the window.

My father heard us opening the window, then came over and started smashing his shovel down all around it. We ran for the door, but my father got there first, so we ran back to the window, then back to the door, and back and forth. We didn't think to try getting out at different places. We were scared and unsure what to do until one of the twins was brave enough to jump out the window. I could hear my brother saying things like, "Oww, that hurts," as my father kicked him. While that was happening, the other twin and I were able to get out the door. The three of us got away and spent the night sleeping outside a little way up the mountain.

I later learned that my middle brother Kobi had also been home that night. He had been in a different room when my father first came in the gate. While the twins and I had stayed inside at first, Kobi had gone out and climbed up on the roof. The whole time my father was chasing the twins and me back and forth between the door and the window, Kobi had been tossing bundles of grass drying on the roof down on my father.

My father was sober when we came home the next morning. The dirt wall of our house showed the damage from each swing he had taken with the shovel the night before, and we could see he hadn't been joking around. There were many large, deep marks around the door and window from swings that could have killed somebody. When we told my father what he had done and showed him all the damage, he claimed he didn't remember anything. He seemed angry that we were showing him the damage, as though he thought we were making it all up. I don't remember him ever taking responsibility for the things he did while drunk. Any time we told him about something he'd done while drunk, he either got angry or was just quiet for a while.

Two of my older brothers, Dukher and Kobi, got fed up with my father getting drunk and trying to beat us. Children are expected to treat their parents with respect in Tibet, but there's a point when enough is enough. One day when my father came home drunk and angry, Dukher and Kobi wrapped him in a blanket and tied him up tight, leaving him like that for the night. The next time he came home drunk he quietly went to bed without causing any trouble. It was better after that for a long time until Dukher got married and moved in with his wife's family. After Dukher left, my father started to go wild again.

As bad as my father was, I'm grateful that my brothers never threw him out of the house. They easily could have; my brothers stayed at home until adulthood and marriage, and my father lives with Kobi now that he is older. In Tibet, older people stay with their families. There are no retirement homes, and it takes a lot of work to cook and maintain a house. I don't know what my father would have done if my brothers had refused to continue putting up with him. It's possible he didn't expect to live long enough for old age to be a problem. My father drank absolutely as much as he could, not once, but many times. He passed out in the road on the way home in the winter many times as well. If no one had found him, he would have frozen.

My father was a broken man who had all but given up on life, but he did have his better moments now and then. One nice thing I remember is him saving the candies for me that he got as change when he bought alcohol. If he forgot to give them to me, I'd take them out of his pockets while he was passed out. I don't know how my siblings feel, but I never hated my father. Mostly I feel sorry for my mother for the position he put her in; she never had the chance to enjoy her own life while doing the work of two parents.

10. A Tragic Turning Point

I WAS FIFTEEN WHEN my parents started thinking about arranging a marriage for me. In Tibet, fifteen isn't an unusually early age to be thinking about marriage. My parents were married at fifteen and so was my sister. I really wasn't ready at that age, but no one asked me what I wanted. I heard my father talking to my mother about friends' sons who might be good matches for me, and I assumed that an arranged marriage was just something that was eventually going to happen.

The rest of my brothers and my sister had already married and moved out, although none of them were very far away. Only the twins and I were still living at home at that time. Normally one of the sons would stay home and bring his wife to live with the family. My parents' plan was that I would stay and my husband would come live with us. My father knew his daughters-in-law wouldn't appreciate his drinking. As he got older he would need more care, and he couldn't depend on an unhappy daughter-in-law like he could his own daughter.

Before any plans for an arrangement were made, something very bad happened. If nothing had changed in my life that year, I almost certainly would have soon been married to a local boy, stayed in my parents' house, and continued with some version of the same life I'd always known. I would be there today and for the rest of my life. What did happen changed that path dramatically.

Every November during the winter lull in farm work, it was the custom for the entire village to take part in a ten-day prayer at the local temple. One member from each family was expected to be present for the entire duration of each of the ten days. There was a small fine to pay if a family didn't send someone. The year when I was fifteen, my mother asked me to go for my family. As part of my obligation for the daylong prayers, I had to get up at four in the morning to go to the temple, and I didn't get back home until well after dark, around ten o'clock. Everyone else would be in bed asleep by then.

At the end of the third day, I came home at the usual time in the darkness. My mother always locked the gate from the inside when the last person went to bed but had left it unlocked for me that night. As I started opening the gate, a person hiding in the shadows grabbed me. I started to yell, and a voice warned me to be quiet. I recognized who it was when I heard the voice. It was an older boy from my village, maybe eighteen years old. He always used to say "hi" when he saw me in the street and tell me I was beautiful. I knew he was interested in me, but I had always ignored him.

He started kissing me, then began to take off my pants. I told him to stop. When I told him I was going to call for my mother if he didn't leave me alone, he replied that I had to be quiet; if I yelled out to my parents he was going to tear my pants.

Looking back on it, I'm embarrassed now that I was so worried about him tearing my pants. It's hard to forgive myself for that. I feel stupid about it, knowing now that there's no way ripped pants would have been nearly as bad as what was coming. At the time, though, I was actually very afraid of my pants getting torn. My family couldn't afford new clothes, and if he ripped the pants I had on, I would have no pants to wear the next day. More importantly, I didn't know what I would tell my parents if I came home with ripped pants. My mother was much better than my father, but I was afraid of both of them. My mother was already so overwhelmed as it was, I didn't know how she would handle one more problem. I was also ashamed; I didn't want anyone to ever find out about what was happening.

I tried to fight him. I tried, but I wasn't strong enough. I lost the fight and was raped. He left when he was done, and I sat down. I tried to think of what I should do next. I thought my parents would be angry with me if I told them what had happened. In Tibet, you absolutely cannot have sex before you are married. I decided I had to keep it secret. After I made that decision, I stayed where I was on the ground for a while. I couldn't hold back my tears for a long time. When I finally went inside, my mother knew I was late, but she didn't suspect anything unusual had happened. She said, "Oh there you are," and we both went to bed. I couldn't sleep at all that night, and at four o'clock I was up to go back to the temple.

Time passed and life went on. Everything went back to normal except that I stopped having periods, and I began to wonder if I was pregnant. I didn't know very much about those things as a girl; it wasn't something parents talked about with their kids, so I kept quiet. After three months without a period, I went to see another girl in the village who I knew was pregnant (and married), thinking she was going to help me understand my situation.

She advised me to smash a ceramic bowl into powder, mix the powder with dust gathered from the wooden beams of the ceiling of our house, add water, and drink. She said doing this would make me lose the baby. I followed her instructions exactly, then I started expecting to see the baby come out any time. Every time I peed, I checked to see if the baby was coming out. It never did work, and I'm probably lucky it didn't kill me either.

Word about my pregnancy soon spread through the village. Within a few days after I told this girl I thought I was pregnant, my mother heard people talking about it. My mother looked very nervous when she came home after hearing that. She looked me in the face and asked me if it were true. I told her I didn't know for sure if I were pregnant or not but hadn't had a period for a long time; then she asked to see my nipples. She said she could tell from their color whether I was pregnant or not. As soon as she saw my nipples, she began waving her arms, slapping her legs, and saying, "Oh my gosh, oh my gosh, baby's coming!" To my surprise, she didn't scold me or beat me; she was totally focused on trying to figure out what to do about it.

She told my father she needed money for medicine for a stomach problem and sent me to the nearest city, Guinan, with one of my sisters-in-law. She asked my sister-in-law to go with me because she didn't know how to find the hospital herself. We walked all day to get to Guinan and spent the night with a cousin who worked as a teacher in the city. My cousin scolded me very badly. I couldn't explain the situation to her, and she assumed I must have been up to no good. She kept poking me in the forehead while saying, "How did you do that?" She asked if I had a boyfriend, and when I said no, she got even angrier.

At the hospital the next day, a doctor felt my stomach and vagina then told us the baby was about three months along. She said she couldn't perform an abortion until the baby was five months along. She didn't say why, just that we would have to wait and come back when the baby was bigger. It was too late to walk home when we left the hospital, so we spent the night at the house of a Chinese friend of my mother. Although my mother's friend was out for a few days when we arrived, her husband and son were there, and they invited us to stay.

For dinner, they made momos with a kind of meat we didn't recognize. We only had experience with pork and goat meat, and we knew it wasn't either of those. My sister-in-law was very worried that it might be dog meat. Some Tibetans say that Chinese people eat dogs, and we were too shy to ask if it were true. On the walk back to the village the next morning, my sister-in-law talked endlessly about what kind of meat we might have eaten the night before. The more she talked about it, the more irritated I got, thinking that there I was pregnant, and she was still worried about the stupid momos.

My mother took the news that I had to wait another two months for an abortion hard. We both wanted to put this behind us, and my mother was nervous that it was going to be difficult to hide the pregnancy from my father, brothers, and other villagers for much longer. She knew my father would be furious if he found out, and it wouldn't be easy to arrange a marriage for me if the rest of the village knew about the pregnancy. There was nothing to do about it, so I tried to wait out the next two months the best I could.

Unfortunately, my mother was right to worry about keeping the pregnancy hidden. My father did find out. Not long after I came back from the trip to the hospital, my father and Kobi took a tractor to Guinan to have some timber sawed into boards. When they were done, they stopped by Yula's house in the city. Someone from the village had already told Yula about the rumors that I was pregnant, and he told my father and Kobi. All three of them were extremely upset.

My mother and I were out working in the yard when my father and Kobi pulled up to our house in the tractor. At first, we didn't know anything was out of the ordinary. My mother asked me to go inside to get some tea for them, then before I could even get inside, my father jumped off the tractor, screaming, "You whore! I heard you are pregnant and you've embarrassed the whole family!" He grabbed a piece of wood as he came through the gate and threw it at me. Kobi grabbed me by the hair and threw me on the ground. He started stomping on my stomach as though he were trying to kill the baby. My father joined him in beating me, both of them kicking and stomping me while my mother screamed at them, "Let my daughter go!" She screamed as loud as she could that they were killing me, loud enough for our neighbors to hear.

As a few people came in the gate to check on what was going on, I was able to get up and run into the house. My father and Kobi chased me inside, closing the door behind them. They continued beating me as much as they could. They looked like they were seriously trying to kill me. My mother had gotten into the house, too. She screamed the entire time this was happening and opened the door for the neighbors to come in. My father and Kobi couldn't keep beating me like that in front of other villagers, so they let up, and I ran out of the house. As I ran, my father yelled out, "You go away! I don't want you coming to my house anymore! Just go away!" Crying, I ran to a neighbor's house. The neighbors treated me very kindly. They tried to comfort me as best they could, telling me that what had happened happened, and we were going to get through it.

I went to stay with my older brother Nyima, who lived in the same village. He wasn't angry with me, only sad. The first night I stayed there was the first time I ever saw him drink alcohol. He is a miserly person who almost never spends money on anything like alcohol that he doesn't really need. I overheard him talking to a friend of his, crying. He said, "So what if my sister's pregnant? I can take care of the baby. Why did my father try to kill her?" It meant a lot me that he wasn't angry. Before I heard that, I thought maybe everyone in my family hated me.

I was afraid to come home for a long time. Nyima told me it was okay for me to stay as long as I wanted—forever if I needed to. My mother came to see me every day to check on how I was doing. She eventually convinced my father to let me come home by telling him she needed my help around the house.

My father held on to his anger for a long time after I returned home, and the twins were not much better. I understood what they were feeling; the situation had become an embarrassment for the whole family. My pregnancy had become the talk of the village, talk focused on everything wrong with me and my family. I could see the gossip was hard on all of us. No matter what my family members did, I can't be angry with them. It was a difficult time for everybody.

My parents both wanted me to have an abortion. First we had to wait until I was five months pregnant; then there was a new problem: My parents no longer had enough money to pay for the procedure. They tried bringing me to a Tibetan doctor who was much cheaper than the hospital. The Tibetan doctor didn't say no, though it was clear he didn't really want to perform the abortion. He told us he had to order a special medical device, and we had to wait for it to come. Every day, we went to ask him if the device had come yet, and each time we saw him, he said it was on the way.

While waiting for the device to arrive, I was staying with Yula. It was terrible staying there. The first thing he said when he saw me was, "What is she doing here? You didn't kill her?" He wouldn't even look at me the entire time I stayed with him.

After two months of waiting, the Tibetan doctor was still telling us the special device was on the way. My father finally gave up and borrowed money to take me to the hospital. At the hospital, the doctor put an injection in my stomach and told us to come back the next day at four in the afternoon. When we returned the next day, they gave me a room and a bed. Around five o'clock I started to have pains. The pain was much worse than giving birth to my two daughters as an adult. This pain went on and on. The nurse left, leaving my family and me alone with no idea what was going on.

The baby came out late that night. The nurse said it was a girl. I could see the baby had a lot of hair. The hair was black or brown. Her head was dark blue. The nurse said the injection was a poison they had put in the baby's head. I remember clearly the dark blue color of the dead baby's head. The baby was big, almost fully grown. It looked pretty much the same as my daughters did when they were born. I don't think I will ever forget that baby in this life. I can still see her blue head with lots of dark hair. I never saw the baby's face.

I wish I had never had that abortion. I still think about the baby sometimes. I think about how old she would be now and what kind of person she would have been. I feel angry with my parents about it. Having an abortion so late in my pregnancy was their decision, not mine. Except for Nyima, people around me had acted like I had a monster inside me, but it wasn't a monster, it was a baby. I'd like to think I would have kept her if I had a real choice. I know my parents didn't have much choice either though; they were thinking about my future.

I started to hate men after the rape. I thought about what had happened to me and thought about my father, and it seemed clear that men only liked to eat, drink, and have sex. I thought men didn't ever think about anyone else or think about how their actions affected other people. It looked like they only thought about their own enjoyment.

I definitely didn't want to marry a man and have a life like my mother's. I saw my mother's life with my father and didn't expect anything better than that if I were to get married. I watched my father come home drunk late at night with his friends and make my mother get up to cook for them all, and I expected that same servitude to play out in my own future.

11. How I Became a Nun

I HAD ALREADY BEEN thinking about becoming a nun for two years before the rape. I learned about nuns from a friend of my mother who sometimes came to visit. The woman was a little older than my parents; she had known my grandmother before becoming friends with my mother. She had been married with several children during the Chinese invasion, during which she witnessed her parents tortured to death in front of her. She left her old life behind to become a nun so she could benefit her dead parents by performing special prayers for their next life.

Around age thirteen, I became interested in becoming a nun as well through meeting her. I already knew my mother would never agree because she needed my help at home, so I asked my father. My father said that only women with something wrong with them wanted to become nuns. He thought the only people who went into a monastery were people with physical deformities or mental disabilities whom nobody wanted to marry. I considered arguing with my father. I wanted to point out to him that my mother's friend didn't have anything wrong with her, but I decided to let it go.

I didn't say anything more about it to my parents for two years. Then, after the rape, I couldn't stop thinking about becoming a nun. When I went to bed, I stayed awake with thoughts of going to a monastery, and when I got up in the morning, it was the first thing on my mind.

Out of concern for my mother, who needed my help through the summer, I waited until fall to take action. Besides her, I didn't worry about what anyone else in the house was going to do without me. After the harvest was in, I went to a small monastery near the village to ask how I could become a nun. The geshe (an especially learned monk) in charge of the monastery didn't seem to think I was serious, but he answered the question. He told me that the first steps to becoming a nun were that my parents needed to agree and I had to get nun's robes.

I came home disappointed because I was sure my parents would never agree, I didn't have any idea where to get the right clothes, and I didn't have any money of my own to buy them. After some thought, I decided to go back to the monastery anyway. This time, I wasn't going to leave until they let me become a nun. I asked a friend if she were interested in going with me and was glad to find she was excited about the idea.

The decision having been made for what to do, we next had to figure out how to do it. Our first obstacle was that we didn't have any money. The only plan I could think of to get money was to steal some from my father. People in my village had never heard of a bank; our habit was to keep money in a locked box. My father kept the key to my family's box in his shirt pocket. One night when he came home drunk, I lifted the key out of his pocket once he fell asleep. I opened the box and found a few hundred yuan inside. I took two hundred out. It was my first time ever holding more than a little small change in my hand.

My friend's mother advised her not to mention the plan to her father until she was already a nun. Her mother believed her father would be happy when she came home as a nun but might say no if she asked for his consent. Her mother wasn't able to give her any money without her father's knowledge, so we stopped at her sister's house across the river on our way to the monastery. Her sister approved of her plan and gave her two hundred yuan. Although we didn't know for sure if four hundred yuan would be enough to get nun's robes for the two of us, we were out of ideas for getting money.

When we left for the monastery, I told my mother I wanted to go do something outside, went out of the house, and kept on walking. I felt sorry for my mother as I walked away, but I would not change my mind. The geshe at the monastery looked surprised to see me again. We told him we had the money for nun's robes and were ready to take our vows, and when he asked where our parents were, we made it clear that we weren't leaving until we were nuns. Everybody at the monastery was surprised. Some of the monks who heard the news that two girls had shown up without parents came over to see us out of curiosity.

We hadn't known enough yet about Tibetan Buddhism to realize our mistake. A geshe is a very knowledgeable and respected figure in Tibetan Buddhism, similar to a Ph.D. in the secular world. But a lama is quite different. Every monastery has a lama serving as its caretaker. Although the lama is assigned little specific authority, he is viewed with universal reverence within the monastery. He is looked to for guidance, and it would be highly unusual for anyone not to follow a lama's advice. When the lama dies, he reincarnates, returning to lead the monastery again. It was the lama, the head of the monastery, who gave the vows for new monks and nuns.

Eager to see the lama, we continued our travel without spending the night. Taking only a piece of bread from the monastery, we walked all day until we approached a village as dusk was falling. I knew that my father's sister, whom I had never met, lived in that village. When we got there, I couldn't decide right away whether we should go see her. Rather than stay with her, our first idea was to sleep in someone's haystack. We found a haystack and lay down, but we couldn't relax. The owner would be there early in the morning to feed the cows and horses. If someone found us before we woke up, it might create a problem. It being a cold night and starting to snow, I decided we needed to visit my aunt.

Though we hadn't met, I'd heard she was a very cranky woman. Someone in the village showed us her house, and a little girl opened the gate when we knocked. We asked if my aunt was home, and the girl brought us in. My aunt looked very old. She looked sick and was indeed cranky. Given her age, she scolded us with remarkable enthusiasm. Tibetan teenagers normally do not go around at night, so she seemed to think we must be very awful kids. To her credit, she did let us stay the night. The daughter-in-law she lived with was much friendlier and made us feel welcome. My aunt's daughter was also there to assist with her care. Her daughter told us not to listen to her because her illness was making her unhappy. We got up early the next morning and left straight after breakfast.

There was snow on the ground when we left, which soon soaked into our shoes. Many people in Tibet did not have decent boots to wear in the snow, and of course I didn't. My clothes were not very well suited to winter either. Although the snow wasn't especially deep, we were quite wet and cold as we walked toward the monastery. We walked all day until we got to Guinan.

We stayed the night in the city with my friend's sister-in-law. Although I had family in Guinan as well, I was deliberately avoiding contact with my own family members, knowing it would be a problem if they discovered my plan. We were lucky her family was there; we didn't have enough money to spend the night in a hotel, and we wouldn't have known what to do in a hotel even if we could have afforded one. We stayed with her sister-in-law's family for two nights. I could tell that it was a nice, loving family, and they made us feel very welcome in their home.

While we were in Guinan, it was a good chance for us to buy the clothes we would need as nuns. We found a monk to ask what to do. All we knew ourselves at that time was that the clothes needed to be red. The monk was very helpful, showing us exactly what we needed. He took us to a place to buy the fabric, told us how much fabric we needed to buy, then brought us to a tailor. We explained our situation to the tailor, who was very understanding. He got started on our clothes quickly and undercharged us for his work, as he could see that we didn't have much money.

The clothes were ready the next morning. We started walking again as soon as we picked them up. The walk to Atso Monastery from the city took about one full day. It was snowing again, and the weather had turned very windy. Before long we were covered in snow. We grew tired walking, we were soaked from the snow, the wind blew right through our thin clothing, and we had not brought anything to eat with us. It was a long day. We finally arrived at the monastery just before dark.

We asked a monk to tell us where to find the lama, and he took us directly there. At first, we didn't say anything when we arrived in the lama's room. We were nervous and unsure what we were supposed to do in the lama's presence. A lama is at least as important to Tibetans as a senator is to Americans. We didn't want to make a mistake, so we didn't say or do anything right away. We were also cold, tired, and had run away from home. I started crying.

The lama invited us to come over closer to him, saying we must be cold and hungry. Before we had said anything about our journey, he mentioned the long way we had traveled. It's possible he could guess from our appearance, but we had said nothing to him yet and could easily have been from a local village. I believe that lamas have a special ability to know about people just from looking at them: their past, their future, even when they are going to die.

Within a short time, the lama made us feel like we were close friends. It was easy to carry on a conversation with the lama. We explained everything about our situation to him. Like the geshe, he wanted our parents to agree before he would make us nuns. We both started crying when he said that, begging him not to send us home. He gave the situation some thought, then told us that it was difficult for him to decide what to do considering we had run away from home. He told us we could stay overnight and he would see what was in his dreams before making a final decision.

The lama's assistant called us to see him the next morning. The lama's dreams had not been bad, and he had done a divination to verify that there would be an auspicious outcome if we became nuns. The divination was done with three dice with special letters on them. He had thrown the dice and seen our future from the letters that came up. Although I could tell he was not comfortable with the circumstances, he agreed to make us nuns based on his dreams and the outcome of the divination. We were so relieved that I started crying again, this time from happiness.

The next thing we had to do was have our hair cut off. The Tibetan tradition for women is to grow our hair as long as it gets, weaving it into long braids. When I came to the monastery, my hair was all the way down to my waist. My friend thought my hair had grown extra long because I have a big head. The last time I'd had a haircut was when I was nine or ten years old, when my mother had cut my hair straight across the top to keep lice out. Older kids made fun of my ridiculous haircut; they said it looked like a donkey had been chewing on my hair. I hadn't wanted another haircut since then, but now I was delighted to have it all cut off.

After an old monk cut off our hair, we put on our robes and took vows from the lama. We stayed in the monastery three days in all, a total of seven days from the time we left home. My mind felt incredibly clear during our stay at the monastery. In the midst all the new experiences that we were facing, I felt calm and peaceful.

Though I was very happy at the monastery, we couldn't stay there forever. For one thing, the residents of the monastery were only monks. For another, we needed to go back to see our families, who we knew would be worried about us. Our hair cut close to our heads and wearing our new red robes, we headed back home. On the way back, we saw a man from our village who had taken his tractor into the city for some business. We addressed him by name and asked for a ride back home. The man looked back at us surprised and confused, thinking we were total strangers. Finally, after some thought, he said our names and asked if we were those girls. We said yes, and still surprised and confused, he gave us a ride.

My mother came to my family's gate when I knocked. For a while, she just looked at me. Her eyesight was so poor she couldn't recognize me with my robes and haircut. Monks and nuns sometimes came around the village in the winter asking for donations for their monastery to do something special like build a chorten (a kind of Tibetan shrine). She must have thought that's what I was doing, because she only stood there waiting for me to say something. When I spoke, I said, "Mom." Finally recognizing me, she screamed, her hand hitting her leg while she shouted, "Oh my gosh! Oh my gosh!" over and over again. For several minutes she only slapped her leg and shouted, "Oh my gosh!" Then she screamed, "You need to run away! Father is very angry!" Seeing that we could not go into my house, my friend and I turned and ran to hers.

Her parents were relieved and happy to see her again. Her father was happy to see her and happy for her to be a nun, even though she had kept her plan secret from him. They let me know I was welcome to stay with them while my father was angry. I'm sure I was truly welcome, but I wasn't comfortable staying there a long time because they already had a large family to take care of. I started going to see my mother from time to time after a few days, and eventually I moved back in with my own family.

My father didn't talk to me for a month, and my mother had

mixed feelings about what I'd done. She was happy that I was a nun, and she was happy I wouldn't have the same problems with married life that she had, but she was also worried about my future. Nuns usually received food from their families, and she was concerned my family wouldn't do a good job taking care of me after she died. My father did eventually come around to accepting me as a nun. He realized that what happened had happened and he couldn't change it.

My friend and I started walking to the nearby monastery every day, the one with the geshe. The walk took a little over an hour each way. At the monastery we practiced meditation and studied Buddhist teachings. The focus of much of our study was on preparations for our next life. We studied and meditated there for about one year, at which point I wanted to go to a bigger monastery where I would be able to receive specialized teachings in meditation. I went to another monastery a little farther away, and my friend decided to stay where she was at the local one.

Although the larger monastery I went to was really for monks, anyone could come to study there. It had a large kitchen with beds for visitors to stay in. A few old men came by regularly, and other people came seasonally to participate in special prayers. I stayed in the big kitchen with the other visitors. Since it was a monastery for monks, I could only stay there for specific teachings and meditations. It would be unusual for a nun and monks to spend long periods of time living together.

I would have been happy to have a permanent residence in a monastery for nuns, but my options were limited by distance from my home. I depended on my family to provide my food most of the year, with the exception of particular periods of religious observance when local communities sponsored the monasteries. I couldn't expect my family to travel too far to bring me supplies. The closest monastery for nuns I knew of would have been a perfect match for me, but it was just too far away.

I attended the special ceremonies and meditations as often as I could. During these special events, monks and nuns could mix in the monastery's large hall. The hall was decorated with many colorful tangkas, or religious paintings, and statues of Buddhist deities. The monks and nuns sat on rows of cushions in the hall, silently listening to the lama or geshe presenting the teaching. The crowded hall was so quiet during the teachings that a single person sniffling a runny nose sounded like a racket. During prayer ceremonies, everyone in the hall repeated a shared mantra for sessions that lasted all day for several days.

The peace of the teaching or meditation would be temporarily broken during meals, when food was brought into the hall. We noisily ate our food. All you can hear from a distance when Americans eat is the sound of people talking while eating quietly. With Tibetans it's quite the opposite. When we eat, especially when drinking tea or eating soup, the sounds of slurping and chomping rise above those of the conversation. At the monastery, just like at home, we typically ate vegetable thukpa.

There was a very peaceful and spiritual feeling inside the hall of the monastery. I really enjoyed being a nun. I didn't have worries about the future or stress to think about, and I liked that I was doing something positive with my life. I could focus on peaceful prayers without having to think about getting money or improving my circumstances. It was a calm, peaceful, and spiritually fulfilling existence. My time as a nun was probably the best part of my life.

12. The Meditation Retreat and the Bad News

I MET ANOTHER NUN at the larger monastery who shared my interest in meditation. We were both interested in completing a special prayer involving one hundred thousand repetitions of a mantra beneficial for the well-being of the whole world, including the dead. In order to complete this, we had to go on a retreat to engage in the prayers without distraction. We decided to stay in a certain cave for the five months the meditation takes. Soon after we started living in the cave, my friend's family, concerned for our health through the winter, asked us to move to a small building they had built nearby for occasional overnight stays when they were in the area following their flock of sheep. We agreed and spent the rest of the meditation time in that little hut.

During the meditation retreat we would get up at five o'clock in the morning and go to bed at midnight. Being winter, it was very dark both when we woke up and when we went to bed. We practiced meditation all day long in between. Nobody was there to check on what we were doing, but we followed the rules strictly; we wouldn't have been doing this if we weren't serious. Three times a day my friend's mother brought us our meals, the only times we could talk. The meals corresponded with when the sun first appeared over the mountains in the east, when it was at its apex, and when it went down behind the mountains in the west. Other than those mealtimes, we could not talk or take breaks. We had to focus completely on our meditation.

After dark, we engaged in a special practice that benefits beings living in the miserable realms. This meditation involves music from horns made from human bone. Where I lived, the dead are thrown into rivers for animals to consume. Monks or nuns interested in this special meditation can find the bones of the dead in the shallows or banks of the river. We use leg bones to make the horns, putting holes in the end where the knee is. Tops of skulls are also sometimes used to hold certain religious items.

These horns made from human bone make a very beautiful sound. The meditation is wonderful to listen to, drawing local villagers out at night to hear us. The villagers enjoyed hearing the meditation even though they couldn't understand the words of the meditation mantra. The beautiful sound of the bone horns moved people to tears without them understanding anything about the meditation itself.

While playing the horns, we envisioned offering our bodies to afflicted beings. I pictured my body like food set out on a table for them and watched them consume my flesh and blood before going away only when there was nothing left. There was always a crowd of the afflicted beings that came rushing all together over to my body offering. They came and ate like starving animals, eagerly swallowing as much as they could.

I had an unusual dream one night while on this retreat. I'll try my best to explain it; it might be confusing to anyone who hasn't lived on a farm. On our farm, we grew almost all of our food ourselves. The only foods we ever bought were salt and occasionally rice. Our fields and animals supplied everything else we needed. If there were a problem with a year's crop, it meant a problem with the year's food supply. It was possible to borrow from neighbors if we had a lean year, but we would have to repay the same amount the next fall.

Our main crops were wheat and barley. Wheat grows fairly tall, just about up to an adult's elbow. When it turns yellow in the fall, the entire stalks are cut as close to the ground as possible with a sickle. After being cut, the wheat is tied into bundles that are stacked next to the house. The seeds are later separated from the stalks, which are saved as feed for livestock over the winter.

Stacking the wheat bundles has to be done exactly right. Building the stack is a job for the most experienced family member. In my family, it was done by my father. My father was an alcoholic, but on this day, he didn't drink anything and always did a good job. The stack was made with the grain on the inside and the bottom of the stalk facing outward. It was extremely important that the stack be properly balanced. If the bottom were too narrow, it would fall over, spilling the seeds. On the other hand, if the bottom were too wide, we would run out of bundles before the top was full. In that case, rain could get in, ruining the seeds inside. This stack held a large part of our food for the year, so we absolutely could not make any mistakes.

In my dream, my brother Dukher was building the stack. I knew that wasn't right. None of my brothers had enough experience; my father should have been doing it. Although he was not as experienced as my father, it looked like Dukher got off to a good start. He almost finished, but the stack was crooked and fell over. One his second attempt, he had the stack almost finished again, only to realize he had made the bottom too wide. There was a small empty space on the top, with no more bundles to work with. It was just big enough to let rain in. That's when I woke up.

I told my friend about the dream during our breakfast break. She was quiet; she knew the dream was bad. I was sure something bad had happened to my family. I wanted to go home to find out what had happened but had already committed to my meditation. Once started, a meditation retreat has to keep going no matter what.

The meditation mantra is received from a special lama. Receiving a mantra includes a vow to the lama to repeat the words every day until the meditation is finished. The vow is absolutely unbreakable. It was not easy for me to keep, even before the dream. Constant meditation made me tired, and it was difficult to spend so much time focused on my mantra without moving around. Every morning I wished I could sleep a little longer. Somehow, despite minimal physical activity, I was rapidly losing weight. I had to reassure myself with the thought that if other people could complete meditations lasting a year or longer, I could do it for five months. The feeling that something had gone wrong with my family was difficult to bear, but I still couldn't quit the meditation. I had to complete my vow.

After she heard about my dream, my friend's mother volunteered to go to see my parents. I couldn't have asked her to do it if she hadn't volunteered; it was a two-day walk over mountainous terrain each way to get to my village and back. I deeply appreciate that she volunteered to do that for me, or else I would have had to continue my meditation for another three or four months without knowing what was going on.

When she came back, I could see on her face that something was wrong before she spoke. I thought maybe someone had been in an accident or gotten sick. I guessed that my mother was sick. It didn't occur to me anyone might be dead. When she told me Prri had died, I was shocked. I couldn't believe it. It didn't feel like it was true. I still had the sense he was out there somewhere.

Though I'd always had an unusual relationship with the twins, I loved them both very much. Zondija and Prri had a close relationship with each other that the rest of us didn't fully share in. They mainly kept to themselves at home and were very shy around people outside the family. There were occasions I saw them fight with each other so seriously that I ran away frightened. Later that same day I'd see them happily together again.

The two of them always shared a bed and a single blanket. As children, if one of them had a bad dream and called out to my mother, chances were the other one was having a bad dream too at exactly the same time. They were so close my mother joked that when they grew up they'd have to share a wife. She said the family didn't have the money to start two households anyway, and if they shared a wife all she'd have to do is make a bigger blanket for three people.

My mother loved the twins more than the rest of us kids. My father was frustrated with them because neighbors often complained about them fighting and making trouble. They were famous in the village for fighting. One time when they were fighting outside our house, they tumbled into a hole we used for storing potatoes over the winter. My father said, "Good, you guys fight in there," and covered the hole until nighttime. It was common for teenagers to fight; the problem was that the twins were too good at it. Tibetan boys who lost a fight would try to fight again and again until they won, but nobody could beat Zondija and Prri. Other parents got fed up because their sons were getting beat so often. The angrier my father got with them, the more my mother loved them. She felt they needed her love more than any of us.

I knew that something was wrong with Prri before he died. He occasionally suffered from swelling, particularly in the mornings. His face would get quite swollen, and then the swelling would go away again. That went on for a few years, and we never thought it was something to be very concerned about. There was no money to take him to a doctor to find out why it was happening. We hoped it wasn't anything very serious and went on with our lives.

Now I have tremendous regret that the family never took him to see a doctor. I can see in America that many problems can be fixed if a person gets medical attention in time. Maybe he could have been saved if we'd had money to take him to a hospital. It makes me sad that here in America pets can get surgery, but my brother couldn't even see a doctor. The last time I talked with Prri, he asked why I had to go away from the family for so long to do a mediation retreat. He thought if I wanted to meditate, I should do it at home. It was probably the nicest thing he ever said to me. He was only twenty-one years old when he died. I feel very sorry for him, my mother, and Zondija.

Near the end, the family could only hear Prri talking about Zondija. His voice was too low to understand what he was saying; the family could only make out that he was repeating his twin's name. My mother said it sounded like he wanted to send Zondija a message.

Zondija had also been away when Prri died, looking for work outside the village. There was no telephone, no mail, and no way to send a message to him until he came back on his own a month later. Zondija almost went crazy with grief when he found out. Exactly one year after Prri died, he also became seriously sick. My family asked a lama what to do to help him, and the lama changed his name, a common remedy in Tibet. When my uncle died from the curse, my father had also gotten sick. When his name was changed, he got better. The name change helped Zondija a little too, though his life has never been the same since.

Before the name change, Zondija's name had been Prachay, but everybody called him Tudung. Tudung means something like "tough guy," or someone who is rough and strong. Nicknames were common in the village. Mine was Nakuma, which means "flat-nosed woman."

When my meditation retreat was complete, I walked home, stopping by my monastery on the way to let them know I was finished and would be ready to begin a group meditation after Losar. Dukher was standing outside the gate as I approached the house. He didn't say anything when he saw me, and I didn't say anything to him; I went straight inside to my mother. My mother started crying as soon as she saw me come in. I could tell right away that the whole family was unhappy. We were all feeling sad, and we all didn't want to talk about it. Maybe we were all feeling guilt and regret that we hadn't taken the illness more seriously all along.

My family didn't have a table for meals. Instead we would sit around the fire together talking about the day, plans for the farm, advice from our parents, and whatever else was on our mind. I'd always enjoyed eating meals like that, surrounded by my family, particularly in the winter when the warmth of the fire was most welcome. Each one of us had a spot near the fire where we always sat. As we gathered around the fire the morning after I returned, there was an empty spot where Prri should have been. Seeing that empty spot, I wanted to wait a while longer for my missing brother to come before starting the meal. My heart was still feeling that he must be on his way. He often watched the sheep for our family; it seemed as though he would be coming back with the flock any minute. As we ate, I looked out the door for him to come home.

Of course, he wasn't coming back. His spot stayed empty that morning, and for every meal that followed. The second day I was home, I still felt like he would come back. Then, after three days, four days, five days, I slowly got used to it. I gradually came to terms with the fact that Prri was truly gone. The full funeral ceremony and ensuing prayers had been completed long before I returned, and there was no grave for me to visit. Keeping with Tibetan tradition, the few photographs our family had with Prri in them had been burned. It was as though he had simply disappeared.

The one good thing that followed Prri's death was that my father began to change his bad habits. He's never said anything about what went through his mind after Prri's death, but it is clear that he was deeply affected by it. Since then, he has cut back on his drinking, and he is making more effort to help the family. Now that he is getting older, he actually has almost the opposite problem of the way he used to be. At a time when people his age are supposed to be spending more time relaxing, he's decided he wants to help the family by taking out the sheep. Although it is a big help for Kobi, who my father is living with, it makes us all worry that my father might have a problem out there some day and there will be no one around to help him.

13. A Tough Year

MY FAMILY WAS already in pain the year Prri died. Dukher's wife had also died earlier that same year. She originally became sick while pregnant. She had gone out to check on her son, who was watching a movie being shown in the village. He was six or seven years old, and she thought he might have fallen asleep at the movie and needed to be carried home. While she was walking in the dark, a whirlwind on the road blew over her. Tibetans believe that some whirlwinds, especially those spinning counterclockwise, are made by ghosts. Ghosts are considered potentially hostile and dangerous, particularly to pregnant women. Our tradition is that pregnant women should avoid going out at night as much as possible. When my sister was pregnant, the family made sure she stayed inside at night and kept the gate tightly closed.

After the whirlwind passed through Dukher's wife that night, she developed a rash and became very ill. First Dukher took her to the hospital in Guinan, and when she didn't improve there, he took her to a bigger hospital in a larger city. It was the farthest from home he had ever been. Having little money to pay for treatment, he had to borrow from everyone willing to lend him even one yuan. He sold everything he could: his animals, his furniture, even his stock of barley. Despite medical treatment, his wife lost the baby and continued to get worse. After a long time in the hospital, she finally died. Before she died, she asked my brother to take her home to die there, since she wasn't improving and knew the family didn't have money for her treatment. Dukher insisted she stay, hanging on to the hope that she would get better.

Dukher and his wife's family brought her body home to her village from the hospital. Seven monks and a lama performed seven days of prayer for her transition to her next life, and the whole village prayed for her for forty-nine days. Whenever there was a death in one of the villages near where I grew up, everyone in that village showed up for such prayers. My father and I went to be with Dukher in his wife's village. My father left after the monks were done, and as a nun, I stayed the entire forty-nine days.

At the end of the forty-nine days, Dukher came back home from living in the other village with his wife's family. The saddest part of the situation was that he couldn't take his son with him. His mother-in-law had begged him to let her keep her grandson at home with her, and he agreed to her wishes. When Dukher came home, he had nothing more than the clothes he was wearing when he walked in the door. He didn't bring so much as a small bundle of personal items with him. He left behind whatever hadn't already been sold to pay for his wife's care for the benefit of his son.

My family gathered some money for him to travel to Lhasa to pray for his wife. Tibetans believe that prayers at holy sites in Lhasa are very powerful and helpful for assuring a good rebirth. My mother had always dreamed of going to Lhasa herself. She used to talk frequently about her wish to go there. I am very proud of my parents for doing this for Dukher even though they didn't have money to spare. It was a big sacrifice for them. They gave up whatever money they could have used to go to Lhasa themselves so Dukher could go instead. My mother did eventually get her chance to go to Lhasa too. One of the first things I did for my parents when I got to America was sponsor a trip for them to travel to Lhasa with Yula.

Dukher was devastated by his wife's death. He loved her very much and had literally done everything he could to help her. He is a good man and a good husband. He and his wife had been a very happy couple. I'd visited them in his wife's village a few times as a child. I saw them often joking and laughing together, something I had never seen with my parents. One night when I was visiting and very young, all of us were sleeping together in the same bed when I was scared by the sound of cats fighting outside. Dukher's wife had held me close to her and asked Dukher to go chase away the cats for me. She was very pretty and always smiling. She was a very lovely woman.

A year after Dukher's wife died, my parents started to think about arranging another marriage for him. He was still fairly young, around thirty years old, but he wasn't interested in another marriage. He wanted to become a monk. He asked me to talk to the lama who had made me a nun to find out if it was auspicious for him to become a monk. After throwing the dice, the lama told me it would be wonderful for him to do so. Dukher would have made a very good monk, but my parents didn't agree with his plan, and Yula came home just to scold him. Yula and my parents thought he needed to marry again to move on. Yula told him that if he insisted on being a monk, he should move far away from the family, because they couldn't bear to see him sad for his whole life.

My suggestion was that we go to India together, and he could be a monk there. He turned down that idea by saying he wasn't educated enough to make a life for himself in a foreign country. He said he couldn't even write down his name, so what was he going to do in India? When he went to Lhasa, I secretly hoped he would cross over to India after all. Instead he got married again. He will probably always miss his first wife, but his new marriage is not bad either. He is a good husband, and his new wife is also very good for him.

We didn't celebrate Losar that year, as is customary when there has been a death in the family. It was a very sad time for us, even as our friends and neighbors were enjoying the holiday. We'd all been through a lot at that time. As my mother put it, "God, why are you punishing us? This family already has a difficult enough situation."

At the end of that year's bitter Losar holiday, it was time for me to go back to my monastery for a three-month group meditation. My father and Kobi gave me a ride there on a tractor. It was our only vehicle, and there was no bus going that way. I brought enough food and material for fire for three months with me. It was a five- or six-hour ride.

The road to the monastery was quite treacherous, and Kobi's experience with the tractor on our farm hadn't prepared him to drive it on mountain roads. The road ran along the edge of the mountains surrounding our valley. It was narrow, in awful condition, and there were no signs directing traffic or providing advance warning of hazardous areas. Mountain roads are a series of continuous turns, and as we went into each one, we had no way of knowing what the conditions were ahead or if there were anyone coming the other way. We had to guess as we went, carefully rounding each curve hoping for the best. It was a bumpy road, made only of dirt and rock. The only maintenance it ever received was from occasional efforts by local farmers to smooth out the road with shovels.

Because the road was so narrow, there was little margin for error. A small mistake on a turn could easily send a vehicle tumbling over the edge. It would be a long way down to the bottom of the tall, steep mountains the road ran along. A swift river flowed through the valley below. It was terrifying to look down from the tractor. Inexperienced in these conditions, Kobi nearly drove off the edge several times. He had a close call on the very first turn, stopped the tractor, took a deep breath, started again, and the very same thing happened on the next turn.

I appreciated that my father and Kobi were doing this for me. The same members of my family who had beaten me so brutally not long before were now taking a huge risk to help me get to my monastery in time for my meditation. If it weren't for me, neither of them would probably have ever gone on such a dangerous trip. Kobi kept going only because he understood my feelings about the meditation. He knew it was important to me that we continue forward or I would miss my chance to take part in a meditation I had made a vow to complete.

We were saved by a lucky encounter. A man on foot headed to a place where he could catch a bus to a larger city was hoping to hitch a ride on the way. He had experience on that road and offered to do the driving. It felt like we had been saved by spiritual intervention. We met him in a very empty place, where we couldn't have hoped to find help if we had been looking. His driving was much better than Kobi's, and we arrived at the monastery safely.

My father and Kobi stayed the night at the monastery then headed back home along the same road the next day. My heart was racing all that day. I couldn't stop thinking about them on that road. Fortunately, they did make it back safely. The way back to my village was an uphill journey, so it might have been easier without the downhill momentum pushing them as they turned corners.

14. Preparing for India

AFTER FINISHING MY three-month meditation, I began to have a strong feeling that I wanted to go to India. I was annoyed with the Chinese government's interference with our practices at the monastery. Representatives of the government came regularly and gave us many rules, dictating exactly what we could and couldn't do. It was frustrating because we were only simple monks and nuns practicing our faith, and that's all we were doing. We weren't bothering anyone or making trouble, so I couldn't understand why the government refused to leave us alone.

We were not allowed to have photos of the Dalai Lama, and were we not allowed to talk about him openly. Sometimes, in the company of trusted friends, we did mention the Dalai Lama. These were only small conversations, like "Hey, do you know the Dalai Lama is in India?" Most of us did not know very much about the Dalai Lama, and the few who did have information were afraid to talk about it. During the Cultural Revolution, entire monasteries had been destroyed by the government, monks had been conscripted into forced labor, religious texts had been burned, and lamas had been jailed. Many lamas, including the one who made me a nun, had been tortured by the Chinese government. When I was a nun in Tibet, the wholesale destruction had stopped, but there was still periodic detainment and torture, constant surveillance, and restrictions. In this atmosphere of intimidation, we heard only small pieces of information about the Dalai Lama and nothing about freedom.

During the initial occupation, these many acts of repression against Buddhist culture included one remarkable event in my mother's village. There were signs in the area around the village indicating the presence of divine beings, including handprints and horse hoof prints embedded in rocks. The significance of these was unmistakable; the prints in the rocks looked exactly like the prints regular humans or horses would leave in mud. Locals believed that the spiritual beings who made the prints lived in mountain caves. Cliffs in the mountainsides throughout this area are riddled with small caves worn away by the elements, most of which are high up the sheer cliff face, inaccessible to humans.

Some caves are lower down, reachable from the ground by a determined climber. People from the village occasionally find religious texts or tangkas in the lower caves while searching for lost goats. Some people leave these items where they are, others sell items they find to Chinese merchants for resale to Westerners. In Tibet we believe that these texts and paintings are the belongings of the same spiritual beings that make prints in solid rock.

At the time of the Chinese invasion, one particular cave very high up the cliff face had been identified by the villagers as the home of a spiritual being. Someone in the village told the Chinese soldiers about this cave, and they built special ladders long enough to climb into it. The ladders had to both reach an incredible height and span across the river below the cliff. Once inside, they found the cave filled with religious texts and beautiful tangkas, along with a bowl and cooking pan. The soldiers brought everything out of the cave and burned the texts and tangkas in front of the villagers. My mother was a witness. It was scary and painful for her to watch this happening. She said she that the tangkas were remarkable. When the fire burned out, there were bits of gold from the tangkas left in the ashes.

There was a local Tibetan man who had been given some authority within the village by the Chinese for his willingness to cooperate with them. This man chose to please the soldiers by making a show out of celebrating the desecration of the items found in the cave. He took home the bowl belonging to the cave dweller, telling everyone, "This bowl would make a good dish for my dog." There were some Tibetans like that who collaborated with the Chinese in return for power or material gain during the occupation, and there are still people like that who inform on other Tibetans to the Chinese police.

Not long after this man used the special bowl from the cave to feed his dog, his family was struck by a series of misfortunes. He and his wife were soon afflicted with a mysterious disease that killed him and then his wife a few days later. Before he died, he realized what he had brought upon himself and panicked. He threw the bowl away in the river, but it was too late. While the forty-nine-day period of prayer for the man and his wife was still in progress, their eldest daughter caught a sickness that left her blind. A short time later, one of the younger daughter's legs was paralyzed. Both of the man's daughters and his granddaughter, the child of the blind woman, became nuns in order to stop their family's misfortune. They were still very famous in the village during my lifetime.

In Tibet, we do not have scientists to examine these mysterious items sometimes found in caves. I know what we believe, but I am also curious about what exactly is going on. It would be interesting to me to know how old the items are, what they are made of, and how it was possible for them to get into the caves. To me, it really does look like spiritual beings put them there. An experienced climber with the very best Western equipment could not have climbed into this particular cave. The cliffs are utterly flat, as though the mountains had been sliced with a knife. There is nothing to grab on to and nowhere to place a foot.

The only time the Dalai Lama was openly mentioned was when

the people from the Chinese government came to give us rules. They said all sorts of bad things about the Dalai Lama. When they criticized the Dalai Lama, it felt as though they were beating us. To Tibetans, the Dalai Lama is like a god. He is very important to our religion and our cultural identity. Just as the world has only one sun, Tibet has only one Dalai Lama. If I could, I would have gotten up to fight the people criticizing him. In no position to fight, I decided to go to India to see the Dalai Lama for myself.

I wasn't exactly looking for freedom at that time; I didn't really know what freedom was. All I knew was that the Dalai Lama lived in India, a few monks from the area had gone there to see him, and I wanted to go too. I thought seeing the Dalai Lama would be the most amazing experience possible. I wouldn't regret going to India for that experience even if it meant I had to die the next day.

I didn't have any experience traveling. I had never been very far from my village; I'd never even taken a bus. My monastery was the farthest away from home I'd ever been. I also didn't have any money. It seemed impossible for me to go to India, but I couldn't stop think-ing about it. After my meditation at the monastery was over, I went home to see my parents, thinking the whole time there that this was not what I wanted to do with my life. I wanted to go to India.

I told my mother what I wanted to do, and she hated the idea. We had all heard that many who try to cross the mountains to India die along the way. She said, "Are you crazy? Don't talk about crazy stuff! How are you going to get to India? You know how dangerous it is. I already lost your brother, what am I going to do if I lose you too?" She cried and told me how much she missed Prri. She said that even if I made it over the mountains alive, there would be no one in India to take care of me and that I belonged with my family.

It's a long way to India from my village, and many people have died on the way or been caught by the government. Being caught attempting to flee into India was little better than death, especially for women. Men who were caught were sent to do forced labor. Around the time I went to India, these men were being sent to clear the way for the railroad that now runs into Lhasa from China. Each person caught had to work for three months, digging all day long in rain, cold, and heat. Prison laborers were given only a small bowl of rice to eat each day. By the time they were allowed to leave at the end of three months of labor, in those conditions with so little food, the men would be almost dead. They were exhausted, far from home, and all their possessions had been stolen.

Most men in that situation turned to crime. They had virtually no other options. They had no money to travel home and no prospects of finding work where they were. There are no social programs for the poor in China and no soup kitchens. People had to steal, or they would die of hunger in the street. If a person were in the middle of the sidewalk in America obviously dying of hunger, there's a good chance people would give that person something to eat or try to help. Someone in the same situation in China would be kicked out of the way.

It is even worse for women. Women who are caught are raped first, then sent to do the same forced labor as the men. Most women don't have a way to get home after their sentences are complete, and they must turn to prostitution to survive. It is a terrible and dangerous profession, but these women have no other choice. Prostitutes in China are extremely vulnerable to sexually transmitted diseases. Most women from the villages turning to prostitution have never seen a condom.

Knowing these dangers, my family refused to let me go to India. They didn't want me to even think about it. I understood their concerns, but I could not stop thinking about India and seeing the Dalai Lama.

Other than the objection of my parents, my biggest obstacle was a lack of money. To get to India, I would need money for travel, to pay a guide to take me over the mountains, and to get me started in India. I had an idea. When monasteries are getting old, the monks or nuns go around local villages asking for donations to sponsor repairs. They knock on every door, explaining which monastery they are coming from, what the donations are needed for, and which lama authorized them to ask for donations. In return for donations, villagers are given photos of the lama and necklaces blessed by the lama. I decided to do the same thing, except I would be asking for donations for myself.

It wasn't entirely unheard of for monks or nuns to ask for personal money. Monks and nuns usually received food from their families, but in some very rare instances a monk or nun didn't have a family, or the family wasn't able to provide enough support. Even though I was embarrassed by the idea of asking for money for myself, I could do it if that was what I had to do to get to India.

I had to figure out what I was going to tell people. I couldn't lie and say I didn't have any family, and telling people I was going to India would be far too dangerous. I could be sent to jail before taking my first step toward India if anyone told the government what I was doing. I decided to say I was asking for donations for a special meditation.

I could only do it far away from my parents' village. I didn't want them to know I was still thinking of going to India, and I didn't want them to be embarrassed that I was asking strangers for donations. It would hurt them that I was begging for money when I had a family taking care of me. I told my parents I was going to visit a friend and that I would be back soon. My mother didn't like to see anyone leave home, particularly since Prri's death. She told me she would miss me and asked me to come home quickly.

The first place I went to ask for donations was an area populated by nomadic herders. It was near a friend's house, which turned out to be very helpful. She knew the people in the area and went with me to ask for donations. Some people gave me small amounts of money, between three and six yuan from each family. Other people gave me butter I could sell later. Some families were very friendly when we knocked on their doors, inviting us inside for tea and a small meal. A few people said, "If you want to do a meditation, go ahead," and gave me nothing. I was incredibly embarrassed when that happened.

That first day I started knocking on doors, I felt like a thief. My body shook, my face was red, and my voice wavered. I've never been so uncomfortable in my life. I wanted to give up and turn around, but I knew if I did I wouldn't be able to go to India. I went around the area near my friend's house for three days and did well. I got a couple hundred yuan and some butter.

Next I went to a different area where farmers lived. In the first place I went, someone I knew was there to help me again. The farmers mostly gave me barley grains I could later sell in the city. My family had also always made donations in the form of grain when monks came around my village. After that, I went to several more farming villages by myself. I was relieved that none of the farmers reprimanded me.

In total I received more than a thousand pounds of barley from the farming villages. I stored my grain with a local family in each village who had been particularly helpful to me. After going around several different villages, I asked one family if I could stay with them for a few days.

The family was very nice to me, but I still kept my real reason for gathering the donations secret from them. Thinking I was doing a meditation, they went out of their way to help me. The father went around all the villages I had been to, picked up the barley I'd left behind, and brought it to the city to sell. He gave me the cash as soon as he got back. I later sold the butter myself. Between the cash donations and the proceeds from the butter and barley, I had one thousand three hundred yuan. That was right around what I thought

I would need to get to India. I could have gotten much more if I'd gone to more villages, but I was very happy to have enough to stop.

I gathered up the money and headed home. At home I kept up the story that I had been visiting a friend, even as I was preparing to leave again. I made some bread for the bus trip to Lhasa in order to avoid spending any money in restaurants, and took some tsampa (flour made from barley seeds) to bring with me across the mountains.

This time I told my mother I was going to a distant monastery for one month. She begged me not to go, crying and telling me how much she'd miss me if I left home for an entire month. I responded that I was a nun and my job was to meditate at the monastery, that I wasn't comfortable being a nun and just hanging around at home. My mother didn't say anything back but kept crying. The next day I walked to Guinan to catch the bus to Lhasa.

I spent the night at Yula's house, and in the morning I stopped by the monastery where I had become a nun. I didn't tell the lama I was going to India. It isn't necessary to tell a lama everything. Lamas already know what people are thinking and going to do before they are told. I only told the lama I was going on a long trip to Lhasa and a little beyond it. I asked him if there was any bad luck in store for me on the way. He said that I was too young for travel but that I would safely reach my destination. He warned me to be careful, said he would pray for me, and gave me a blessing necklace.

I was elated to hear the lama's words. If the lama had told me that something bad would happen during the trip, I absolutely wouldn't have gone. I was afraid of being raped, and I did not want to die. I was worried about what would happen to my mother if I died. As it was I knew that what I was doing would be hard on her. If the lama had predicted bad fortune, I was planning on really going to the monastery I'd told my mother I was on my way to. After that I would do the one–year meditation as I had told people I would while asking for donations.

After speaking with the lama, I went to see my old teacher and told him the truth about my plan. He thought my plan was too dangerous, but when I made it clear I was determined to go, he didn't try to stop me. We talked about my reasons for going to India. I said I wanted to go to India to see the Dalai Lama and learn about Tibetan history, and then after three years I would come back to my family. He gave me a donation of one hundred yuan, which was very generous and helpful. Although I didn't make it back to Tibet after three years as I'd planned, I did see my teacher again. Five years later he also came to India.

After spending the night at the monastery, I went back to Yula's house to get my belongings. I was surprised to find my mother waiting there. I had told Kobi about my plan to go to India. Although he thought it would be great for me to see the Dalai Lama, he said I also needed to think about what I was going to do to support myself in India without family around. I hadn't listened to his advice, so he told my mother what I was up to.

When I came in the door, she started crying, "Please, you cannot do this. What am I going to do if you go to India without me?" It was a complete shock to see her. She was always so busy, I couldn't believe she had followed me all the way to the city. I had to lie to her, insisting I was really only going to the monastery for one month. After some convincing, she started to believe me. She said she would wait for me there at my brother's house, and when I returned to the city, we'd go back to the village together. I said that was a good plan. I knew she wouldn't really wait around the city for a month.

I went to get the bus the next morning after breakfast. My mother came with me. She told the bus driver to help me because I'd never been to a big city before. When I sat down on the bus I couldn't believe I was really going through with my plan. I wondered if I could really do it. The bus started to move, and I waved goodbye to my mother. As I looked out in the direction of my village, the familiar landscape falling farther and farther away, the finality of what I was doing sank in. I was really leaving my village and my family, and I didn't know for sure if I would ever be back. I started crying right there on the bus.

I had to switch buses in the next city. As soon as I got off the bus, I went to look for a cousin who lived there. I asked my cousin if I could stay with her overnight, telling her the partial truth about my plan: that I was going to Lhasa. She was happy to let me stay overnight and happy that I was going to Lhasa. I spent the night in the family's only bed, sharing it with my cousin, her husband, and their two kids. The next morning, her husband put all my belongings on his bicycle and gave me a ride to the bus station.

I took the second bus to a place where I could catch a bus to Lhasa. I waited on the road for the bus to come by. A couple buses did go by without stopping for me. From what I'd seen in the past, people trying to catch buses usually waved as the bus approached, and I was waving my arms and jumping to get the bus driver's attention as much I as could. After two buses passed right by despite my vigorous waving, I was confused and unsure what to do.

It was getting dark and cold, so I went to take shelter at a restaurant. A man at the restaurant told me I should make a sign that said "Lhasa" in large Chinese letters or bus drivers might think I was going on a local trip. I found a piece of discarded cardboard and asked a stranger to write the Chinese letters for me, which I had forgotten how to do myself.

I stood along the road holding that piece of cardboard for a long time. While I waited, a man approached me and asked if I was going to Lhasa. I said I was, and he told me he was going to Lhasa too. He was a businessman from Lhasa traveling in my area for sales. At first I didn't trust him. We couldn't communicate much since his Lhasa dialect and my Amdo dialect were completely different. It was my first time meeting a person from Lhasa and my first time hearing the Lhasa dialect. He knew just enough of the Amdo dialect to make an effort to communicate with me using the few words he knew. He asked me to speak slowly to make it easier for him to understand.

He was very friendly, and I started to trust him. I was very happy to have another Tibetan on the way to Lhasa with me. Another bus finally came, and this one stopped, thanks to my cardboard sign. When we got on the bus all the seats were taken, so we had to sit in the aisle. We missed the opportunity to take the first seat that opened up. He tried to send me to sit because I was a nun, and I told him to take it because he was older. While we talked about it, someone else jumped in front of both of us. My new friend put my head on his shoulder and told me to try to get some sleep.

The bus trip continued overnight, then stopped on the way during the middle of the next day. We were in a big city full of Chinese people. I saw huge factories belching smoke and wondered what they were. To me, smoke coming out of a chimney meant someone was cooking. I marveled at what could be cooking that would create such a massive amount of smoke. I wasn't happy to stop there. I thought the bus was going all the way to Lhasa, and I'm pretty sure that it was supposed to. However, the driver wanted to stop and told everybody we'd have to catch another bus the next morning, and there wasn't anything to be done about it. My new friend from Lhasa said it was good to stop because it would be a chance to take a break and clean up.

Watching a group of people wearing chubas get off the bus and head into the city, I wanted to quickly go follow them. The chubas meant that the people were Tibetan, and I thought it was best to stick with the other Tibetans while in this strange city. My new friend refused to go after them. He said that I couldn't trust just any Tibetan. If I wanted to follow them, he wasn't coming with me. I had to think about it a minute. I did want to stick together with the other Tibetans, and I also didn't want to lose this person who was nice and helping me. I decided to stay with the person I was with.

He got a taxi to take us to a hotel and paid for separate rooms for each of us. It was the first time I'd ever been in a hotel. It was necessary to show an identity card to get a room, which I didn't have. Without his help I'm not sure what I would've done that night. He made sure our rooms were next to each other, and he told me to yell for him if anyone knocked on my door during the night.

His room had its own bathroom. It was the first time I ever saw a toilet and a shower. I had never seen anything like it before. Not knowing what these things were, I turned down his offer to let me use the shower. When I needed to pee, I was too embarrassed to ask him how the toilet worked. I tried to figure it out on my own. After I finished peeing I could see that it wasn't going down. I was a little worried that maybe I'd peed in the wrong place. I saw a button and pressed it to find out what it did. The toilet made a loud noise, taking me by surprise. I thought I must have broken it. I got out of the bathroom and kept quiet about what had happened in there. I hated this bathroom. I liked going out among the trees in my village much better. There's nothing complicated in the trees, and it's peaceful to be out in nature.

Looking out the window of the room, I could only see the road and buildings. The entire view was a landscape of concrete. There was nothing green and nothing natural. I started to feel sad and missed home. I started crying. My friend saw me crying and began digging in his suitcase. He pulled out a photo of the Dalai Lama he had hidden in the suitcase rolled up in his clothes. Impossible to buy in Lhasa, he had made sure to bring a Dalai Lama photo back with him from his travels. He said that when he got home he would have to hide the photo behind something else, but he would know it was there. Seeing the photo of the Dalai Lama did make me feel better.

Once I'd started feeling better, he said we should go out and see the city. He ordered a taxi, and we went to a large shopping area. I took my first escalator ride there. He took me around a few places, and he could see I'd never been to a big city before. He told me I'd have to buy my own bus ticket the next day, but otherwise I didn't have to worry, he would pay for the hotel and our food. I shared the bread I'd brought from home with him. He loved the bread and ordered several bowls of soup to eat with it.

The next morning we got on another bus to Lhasa. This time we got our own seats. I told my friend during the ride to Lhasa that I was planning to escape to India. I trusted him and hoped he would offer some advice or be able to help. He warned me not to tell anyone else. He said Lhasa was full of informants for the Chinese police. I noticed some of the Chinese people on the bus using oxygen bottles to breathe as the road climbed up into the thin air of the high mountains when we were getting close to Lhasa. The altitude didn't affect us, so I couldn't figure out what they could possibly be doing. We arrived in Lhasa shortly before lunchtime the day after we left.

One of my brothers had a friend living in Lhasa. Though I'd never met him, I was hoping I could find him and that he would let me stay with him until I found a guide for the trip into India. My friend on the bus offered to let me stay with his family if I didn't find my brother's friend. He also said that he would help with finding a guide.

It was easier to find my brother's friend than I had expected. There is a popular market in Lhasa that many people pass through, and the residents of Lhasa originally from Amdo tended to all know each other. We soon found the address we needed by asking around at the market, and my bus friend took me there. I didn't know what my brother's friend would say when I showed up at his door. He turned out to be very welcoming and a helpful contact for me. When I told him my plan, he tried to discourage me from going, telling me all the dangers I would face on the way. He thought it would be best for me to see the sights of Lhasa and then go home.

I listened to what he had to say but insisted that I'd come this far and was serious about going all the way to India. Once he saw he couldn't change my mind, he told me he knew of a group of Tibetans leaving for India that very same night. He was a friend of the guide, and he had gone over the mountains before himself. He took me out to get clothes for the trip, as well as a blanket and backpack. His wife and daughter gave me a few of their personal items, including a pair of gloves. Unable to communicate in words because of the difference in our dialects, the daughter pretended to shiver as she handed the gloves to me.

15. Escape

FOR THE LONG, dangerous journey to India, the honesty and competence of the guide was a matter of life or death for the entire group. There were some dishonest guides who took people's money, brought them to a remote spot far away from the city, and disappeared after a few nights. When that happened, people had no idea how to get back. Leaving a group lost in the wild like that was little better than outright murder. There were also honest guides who were simply less skilled than mine. Under our guide's leadership, our group was among the most fortunate: We did not lose a single life.

The group was leaving at nine o'clock that night. I had been in Lhasa no more than six hours when a taxi arrived at my brother's friend's house to pick me up. I had only two regrets as I got in that taxi. The first was that I wouldn't be able to say goodbye to my friend from the bus. He was a very sweet person, and he had helped me tremendously. I wish that I could get in touch with him again. I'd like to thank him for everything and let him know I'm safe. My second regret was that I hadn't seen the Potala, the former residence of the Dalai Lama. I wasn't interested in touring the city except for the Potala, and it had been closed for the day when I arrived.

The taxi dropped me off in a dark place deep in the woods. There was a truck waiting there, the kind used in China to transport commercial goods. The taxi driver whispered to me to get in the truck and left. It was too dark to see inside the truck as I climbed in, but I could tell there were already a number of people inside as I bumped into them. I found a place to sit down and took off my backpack. Inside it were ten pounds of tsampa, some butter, a thin blanket, and an extra pair of pants. I was wearing a regular shirt and pants rather than nun's robes for two reasons: convenience while climbing and because I knew that monks and nuns could expect to be singled out for special harassment if we were caught. Half an hour later the truck departed.

The truck's open bed was covered with canvas. Under that canvas, thirty-five of us squeezed together. We couldn't move at all. We couldn't even stretch out our legs. Cramped as we were, we did our best to sleep that night as the truck took us deep into the wild. The morning sun revealed the faces of the other members of my group, though none of us talked much on the truck. It wasn't until we were on foot in the mountains and spending nights together that we started to have much conversation. It looked like everyone had a friend in the group except for me. When I started talking to people, one man was surprised that I was a woman. He'd seen my short hair and assumed for days that I was a man.

The truck stopped for our first break at the end of the first day. We were in a very remote place, and even so, the break was kept quick. We made tea and ate tsampa, then got right back in the truck. We continued riding for a total of four days. We were startled awake one night by the driver yelling for us to get out. It was the middle of the night and completely dark. Not only were we sleepy, we had hardly moved for days, and there were no flashlights to help us climb out of the truck safely. All we could do was jump out and start moving. The ground we landed on was hard and bumpy. Since we hadn't been able to move our legs during the truck ride, it was difficult to suddenly jump out of a truck. Our legs were stiff and our feet were unstable. I fell down repeatedly while trying to keep up with the group. Each time I fell, I wished I could stay and rest just a little before going on. I would've stayed on the ground if I'd had a choice, but the group was moving, and I knew I needed to keep going with it. In the darkness, no one would see if I fell behind.

We pushed on all night until we reached a valley in the morning. There was a river that ran through the valley and a bridge over it guarded by Chinese soldiers. We couldn't use the bridge, and we couldn't let the soldiers see our group. We had to keep going farther down the river until we could find a good place to cross a safe distance from the bridge.

When there have been recent rains in the mountains, the river can become impassable except at the guarded bridge. If we hadn't been able to find a place to ford the river, our backup plan was to wait until very late at night, then run across the bridge. On the other side we'd spread out and regroup farther on. We were supposed to keep going in the night until we reached the other side of the first mountain, or else it would be easy for soldiers to spot us as we climbed up. Although we could expect the soldiers to be asleep during the night, their dogs would be certain to wake them up. Once the dogs started barking, there would be little time before the soldiers came out shooting. If it came to that, the guide told us to stop running and lie down on the ground until the gunfire stopped. Once the soldiers were done firing into the surrounding darkness, they probably weren't going to come out with flashlights checking for people on the ground.

I met a Tibetan woman in America who had been in a group that went across a bridge this way. She survived, though she was hit by a bullet in her calf. She'd had to walk all the way to Nepal with a leg injury that became badly infected by the time she arrived. In Nepal she met someone from America who sponsored her for a refugee visa. The same person and his family also sponsored her to attend college, and now she is doing well.

Most of us in the group didn't know how to swim. One of the men could swim, making it his job to find a safe place for the group to cross together. He'd look for places where the river spread out the widest and jump in to check if the water were shallow. On the first few tries, he had to come running back to the small fire we'd built hidden behind an embankment to warm up. Other men in the group rubbed his hands and feet to help him recover. The man testing the water was mainly worried about his private parts freezing, but no one was going to help him with that.

We were stuck waiting by the river for two days while we looked for a place to cross. It was taking a long time because we could only come out to check the river at dusk. Dusk was the only time of day when we could see the river but weren't likely to be seen by the local shepherds. On the third day our guide said this was our last chance: If we didn't find a place to cross that day, we would have to go back to the bridge. We couldn't afford to waste our supplies at the river any longer. Fortunately we finally found a place to cross. We were very lucky we didn't have to take our chances at the bridge.

We crossed the river's freezing and swift whitewater holding hands, tied together with a rope brought by our guide. In groups that didn't bring a rope, everyone had to cross individually. It would have been easy for an individual to slip and get swept downriver. There's a good chance not everyone in my group would have made it across that river alive if we hadn't been tied together.

The men in the group stripped down to their underwear while crossing in the hope of keeping their clothes dry in their packs. Being a nun, I couldn't take my clothes off in front of all these men, so I had to cross with my pants on. When I got out my pants were frozen stiff, so stiff I could barely walk in them. We started climbing up the mountain as soon as everyone was out. Wet and cold, it was better for us to keep moving.

The only other woman in the group besides me was much older than the rest of us; I'd guess she was around seventy years old. I'd been reassuring myself that if a seventy-year-old woman was brave enough to do this, I could do it too. The woman started to get sick as we climbed up the mountain after crossing the river. Stopping for her to rest and recover wasn't an option. We had to keep going, all of us doing what we could to help her along.

When I was a nun, it seemed that every time I faced a great difficulty the situation always turned out well. I think of the man who drove my brother's tractor to my monastery over the dangerous roads, the family that helped me gather all my barley to get the money to go to India, the friend I'd met on the bus to Lhasa, and my skillful guide as blessings. It's hard to say for sure that all of these things amounted to anything more than happy accidents, but the improbability of it all gives me something to think about.

This old woman's determination clearly would not be enough to carry her all the way across the mountains, and she could expect almost as much difficulty turning back. It looked like she would not survive the journey. Our entire group would also be in danger from any delay and the extra effort of helping her, yet we would not have considered leaving her behind. Then an extraordinary, unlikely thing happened. We found a small pack of horses roaming out on the mountain. Our group was large enough to surround and catch them. Most Tibetans are very experienced with horses, particularly nomadic herders. I'd always been intimidated by horses myself, but all the men in the group knew what they were doing. They rounded up the horses, and we used them to carry our packs and the old woman.

We continued walking all day and all night with the old woman on a horse until we came to a high mountain that required climbing its jagged rock face. The horses could go no farther. The old woman was getting sicker by this time and suffering from the high elevation. She had no choice but to turn back. A friend of hers in the group volunteered to go with her. I assume that they were able to get back to Lhasa safely on horseback. The rest of us continued onward to India without the horses.

Sometimes we crossed over the mountains in the daylight. Other times we had to hide during the day and walk at night. We had to avoid being seen by the shepherds who lived in small villages throughout the mountains. If we were spotted, they could report our group to the government for a bounty. We could see their flocks of animals from far away any time we were near a village. Whenever we saw a flock of sheep or yaks in the distance, we had to start walking only at night.

We'd spend those days hiding in ravines. I hated the hiding because the men would invariably pass the time talking about sex. There were several men in the group who had been monks in Tibet and had given up their robes shortly before leaving for India. Several of them had been brought to their monasteries when they were very young, where they'd spent their lives so far uninitiated in worldly subjects. The former monks had endless stupid questions about women and sex that they asked the other men. I hated being around that because I was a nun and because I hated sex altogether at that point in my life. I always went off away from the others to avoid their conversations. When I went away from them, the men would say they understood I was a nun but it was okay for me to stay with them; they said they didn't expect me to take part in the conversation and I could think about something else if I wanted.

There was no trail guiding our journey. We were traveling through a vast and empty expanse, often at night, with no path or landmarks to direct us. It was up to the skill of our guide to get us to our destination. We each brought only enough food to last until we reached the other side of the mountains, so getting lost even for a short time would have been disastrous. I really do feel fortunate for the skill of our guide. He did an excellent job getting us through safely and quickly.

On our first very high mountain, my shoes slipped hopelessly on the ice. I couldn't climb at all. The people behind and in front of me tried to hold me up, but it wasn't working. It soon became obvious that I wasn't going any farther with those shoes on. I was facing the bleak prospects of either turning back on my own or continuing with the group barefoot.

If I turned back alone, my only chance to survive would have been to look for the nearest road and surrender myself to the Chinese. If I had continued on barefoot, I would have certainly suffered extreme frostbite, very likely leaving me unable to walk while still on the mountains. Later I met many Tibetans in India who had lost toes to frostbite from crossing these mountains. A few people lost all their toes. My good fortune came through again to solve the problem: Someone in the group had brought an extra pair of shoes. They were warmer than what I'd been wearing, and they gripped the ice very well. Wearing those, I was able to continue.

We crossed over the snowy mountaintops in a tight line. We had to exactly follow a narrow path of packed snow left behind by other groups that came before us. The unpacked snow just off the path was very deep. Anytime I took a step off the packed trail my entire leg sank into the deep snow. It was a very discouraging feeling whenever that happened; I was so tired I barely had the energy to pull myself out again. A step over the edge while crossing a ridge could send a person tumbling down the mountain into the deep snow. Climbing back up the mountain through the snow would be nearly impossible, and there was no way for anyone to help. My group crossed over this terrain in September when there was new snow covering the area. In India I heard from people who had crossed the same area in the summer and seen the bodies of our fellow refugees who had made some fatal error.

Our progress over the mountains was slow and arduous. I grew more exhausted by the day. It was demoralizing to put every bit of energy I had into climbing over one mountain only to find another one on the other side. They seemed endless. Each time we got over a mountain, I wished it were possible to say that one was it. I wanted to cry after each one. I found it a little easier to keep going if I didn't look up while climbing. Looking up the mountains, they appeared to rise straight into the air. By climbing on my hands and knees, I didn't have to look at that and be depressed by seeing how much of the mountain was left to climb; I could just focus on moving.

It was bitterly cold in the higher elevations. We didn't have any of the amazing equipment and special clothing Westerners have for mountain climbing. Most of us hadn't even known what to prepare for with the resources we had. My clothes were worn and not nearly warm enough for the conditions. I didn't have a hat, and I'd foolishly left my warm gloves back at home. I had to wrap a scarf around my head in place of a hat, and the gloves I'd been given in Lhasa were made of only thin cloth with no padding. Those gloves were still much better than nothing; I was lucky to have them. While constant walking helped diminish some of the painful freezing in my toes, my fingers were impossible to keep warm.

To make the most out of our thin blankets, we slept in groups of eight with some blankets spread under us and the rest spread out over each group. We slept packed close together in a line, positioned with each person's feet next to the heads of the people beside them. We stuck our neighbors' feet under our armpits for warmth. We didn't care that the feet tucked into our armpits were disgusting. Our jackets went over our heads. Thin sheets of ice formed on the jackets over our faces during the night from the moisture in our breath. In the morning there would be inevitable half-serious jokes claiming someone in the group had spent the entire night kicking someone else in the face.

One of the men made the mistake after sleeping next to me of mentioning that I was hot, meaning warm to sleep next to. The other

Me with two of my group members on the way to India.

men joked about that for a long time, implying he was hot because he was excited about sleeping next to a woman. Joking and singing helped us endure through the cold and difficulty. During our breaks, we always joked and made fun of each other. The slowest person in my group made up for his slowness by being the best singer. He often sang Tibetan folk songs as we walked. My favorite song was one about the peaceful sound of sheep and the beauty of their wool flowing like waves when they move.

Kicks to the face and all, our guide's smart layout for sleeping was an important reason our entire group made it over the mountains alive and without serious frostbite injuries. A roommate I had in India had crossed the mountains in a group where everyone slept on their own. For them, sleeping was the worst part of the day. They shook with cold all night, waiting for daylight just so they could get moving again. No matter how tired they got, she said it was better to keep going than to freeze at night.

Once a day we boiled water to drink and mix with our barley flour. At high elevations, there was no vegetation to make a fire with, forcing us to improvise by mixing our barley flour with snow. I like tsampa, but the limited diet made me sick after so many days of eating nothing else. I was having painful episodes that felt like diarrhea but never produced anything.

By the time our tsampa ran out, our guide promised us we were getting close to a village that was over the Nepalese border. It was exciting to be getting close to the end, but I knew it was going to be a struggle to finish the last few days. Tired and weak, we all looked thin and worn out, like we could be knocked over by the slightest poke of a finger. Going into that final stretch, I shook my tsampa bag and licked the last dusting of flour off my hand. A friend in the group asked me to shake it for him too, and I coaxed every last bit out of the creases for him. It was almost nothing, but even the faint flavor of food was comforting.

After our food ran out, all I could think about was bread. I didn't think about my favorite foods or dream of complicated meals, just bread. I pictured my whole family sitting together around the fire with a huge plate of bread in front of us. My fantasy meal was exactly how I remembered a typical breakfast at home.

One day away from the Nepalese village, we spent the night in a small rock building. It was made of many flat rocks stacked together to make four walls, with an opening for a door and wood piled on top for a roof. There were no signs of use. In a grassy area, I would have thought it was made by shepherds to spend the night when they were far from home with their flocks. In this barren place, my only guess is that it was used by smugglers. Whatever its purpose, we were glad to find it. The night in the rock house was our most comfortable night since we started. We smashed the wood from the roof into kindling and made a small fire. Sitting by the fire with hot water to drink was much better than sleeping out in the open. Outside that small house, we could hear the loud howling and whistling of mountain winds all around us.

16. Welcome to Nepal

WE REACHED the Nepalese village late the next afternoon. On the route we traveled, we entered Nepal somewhere in the area around Mount Everest. We had been walking for one month and three days. The village was made up of only a few families living together in the middle of a desolate landscape. They lived by farming the rocky ground and keeping a few different kinds of animals. Their houses were made of rock with wooden floors. People in the village slept on the floor, with no furniture in the houses and few possessions beyond the basic essentials for cooking.

They appeared to be happy, friendly people. I enjoyed watching the children sneaking around to look at us from the safety of their hiding places, and the men in my group were excited to see the women. For a little money they fed us some of their simple food. It wasn't the best food, just rice and potatoes, but it was extraordinary to us. One man in my group joked that the villagers might be scared to see people eating as much food as we did.

We passed through more villages as we went on. The villages got bigger and had more to offer. Some villages had small stores where we could buy candies. Staying in the villages was a huge improvement over our earlier experiences in the mountains. We were very happy to have food and not be freezing every night. Ironically, I started to feel more tired than ever once we had food and shelter. My mind and body started to relax with the knowledge that we were out of China and past the most difficult and dangerous parts of the journey. My pace steadily slowed down, so in spite of my determination to be one of the first people in my group to reach Kathmandu, I ended up in the back.

The wide–open spaces we'd started in turned into rough trails, which turned into paved roads. After crossing over one final bridge we arrived in the outskirts of Kathmandu. It was strange to us to be in the big city with its crowds and busy shops. The locals thought we were strange too. People on the streets stared at us as we walked along the road. The plan was to walk to the closest bus station and catch a bus to the offices of the Tibetan government in exile. As far as I was concerned, we were out of danger and our journey was virtually over. Once we arrived at the bus station, I expected to just ride the bus to freedom. It was an exciting feeling.

I didn't see exactly what happened at the front of the group on our way to the bus station. When I caught up, I saw that our guide and other men from the group were being confronted by a few Nepalese police officers. Following a tense exchange with the Nepalese police that I couldn't understand, our guide turned to us and said the police were planning to take us to jail and possibly hand us over to the Chinese government. He advised us to ignore them and keep walking toward the bus station.

The officer in charge got on a radio to arrange backup, and before long we were surrounded by Nepalese police with their guns drawn. Seeing those police surround us was a moment of extreme disappointment. We had come so far and been through so much suffering, and now it looked like we would be sent back to China just when freedom was within sight. It was a really awful, sinking feeling to find ourselves in that situation.

Two men in the group had already lived through a similar experience. They had been caught shortly after arriving in Nepal and sent back to China once before. Dumped in Lhasa after completing their labor sentence, they'd had nowhere to go but to attempt to flee into India again. Our guide had felt sorry for them and agreed to take them for free. At the beginning of the trip, the guide had told us all about their situation and asked us to share whatever extra food and warm clothes we had, since the men had didn't have money for their own supplies. We all shared what we could, though the men were shy about asking for anything.

One of the former monks looked around at the police surrounding us and declared that he was not going to go back. He said he would rather fight with these police knowing he would die than let them hand him over to the Chinese government. He told the rest of the group that we could do what we wanted, but that was his choice. Other people in the group started to say, "Me too," right away. One by one, we all said we were ready to die.

Our guide yelled out to the police that if they wanted to give us to the Chinese they were going to have to kill us all. The men carried knives with them, some of them huge. The men pulled out their knives, and I looked around to try to find a weapon for myself. I was looking for a rock or anything hard, without any luck. I didn't matter. I knew that even if I found a rock, the Nepalese police would kill me with their guns before I could use it against them anyway.

It was the first time I really thought about the possibility that I might die on the way to India. I had known it was unsafe from the start, and there were any number of times I could have died, but I hadn't thought much about it. In this situation, I was 100 percent sure that this was it. We had weapons and we weren't going to give up. The men were taunting the police, gesturing threateningly at them with their knives. They held up their knives and pointed to individual policemen, shouting, "Hey you, come on!" in Tibetan. Meanwhile the police had guns already pointed in our direction. It looked like there was no way to get out of that situation alive.

My thoughts turned to my mother. I felt very sorry for her. First she had lost Prri, and now I was going to die too. The worst part was that she would never find out what had happened to me. I hadn't thought about home much through all the cold and the hunger, but now I realized how much my decision to come to India was going to hurt my mother, and I felt bad for leaving my family. However, given that it was too late to unmake my choices, I agreed with the decision of the group. I was ready to die in the street in Kathmandu rather than be handed over to the Chinese government.

To everyone's surprise and relief, the Nepalese police pointed down their weapons. They saw we were truly ready to die and decided to make a deal. They wouldn't gain anything by killing us; we were only worth money to them alive. The police offered to give us a place to sleep for the night and take us to the Tibetan government offices the next morning. Under the circumstances, we were ready to agree.

Our guide told us that the Tibetan government would be charged for the rooms if we went with the police for the night, and we were used to sleeping outside anyway, so we should spend the night on the street instead. He said that if the Tibetan government paid for rooms for us, we would be taking money from the Dalai Lama. We didn't want to take any money away from the Tibetan government, so we all agreed to sleep on the street. The Nepalese police said that was fine and they would come get us in the morning.

We were settling in for the night on the street when someone in the group suggested we pool our money together and get a cheap hotel room. We got two rooms for the group. With more than thirty people in two small rooms, there were people sleeping anywhere they could fit. The police showed up at the hotel with a bus the next morning. They had obviously been watching us—they knew exactly where to find us even though we were in a different place than where they'd left us.

The police claimed they had reached a deal with the Tibetan government. They said the bus would take us to the Tibetan government offices, where they would be paid by the head for our release. We agreed and got on the bus. There were three policemen standing inside the bus with us and several police cars following behind it. A few people said some of us should give up our seats to make nice with the police, but the rest of the group didn't like the idea. We thought the police were bad people and deserved to stand.

Our guide told us not to trust the police. He was familiar with Kathmandu and watched out the window to make sure they took us to the right place. After ten or fifteen minutes he realized the bus was not headed to the Tibetan offices—we were on the road to the local jail. We didn't take that news well. A few men rushed to the front to grab the driver and stop the bus. The three policemen on the bus fought with the men grabbing the driver while yelling out for the other police to come help them.

The policemen had thick wooden clubs to beat us with, the kind Indians call lathi sticks. We couldn't get out the bus door because the three policemen were standing by it, hitting anyone who came close to them. Someone got the idea to kick out a window, and other people soon did the same to all of them. We started climbing through the windows and jumping out. The first people who jumped out helped the others down. One man got stuck in a window and had to be pushed the rest of the way. A few of the men pushed through the police guarding the door, taking their beating as they went out. I went out a window.

We could have gotten out a lot faster if we'd been organized, taking turns. Instead we were all trying to get out at the same time, bumping into each other and getting in the way. The good thing was that when we got out, we all stuck together. If a few people had decided to run off on their own, there's a reasonable chance they could have escaped successfully, but not one person tried to do that. We were all in this situation together, for better or worse.

Outside the bus we were completely surrounded by police, the sirens of many police cars wailing all around us. A large crowd of people gathered on the street to watch. It must have looked pretty exciting. Later in the Tibetan government offices we saw pictures of some of the group members on the front page of the newspaper.

All of us closed in together and sat down, grabbing on to the people next to us. The police tried to break us up by hitting us with their sticks and kicking us. They pulled us apart, two policemen grabbing each person one by one. Every time the police grabbed someone, we held on to that person as best we could. We held on to the person's feet and hands until the last second. The police tried to stop us from holding on to each other by beating the people grabbing on to the ones they were dragging away. After being separated from the group, we were put into individual police cars, two of us per car.

All the police cars went to the same destination, the local police station. When we arrived, they marched us in single file past two guards stationed at the sides of the door. Both guards kicked each of us in the butt as we were thrown inside. They were remarkably adept with their toss–and–kick technique, as though it were a well-rehearsed official police drill. Inside we found ourselves together again in a large holding room.

The first thing the police did after they had us inside was to search us for money and weapons. Following the advice of our guide, we had all sewn our money into our clothing, and the police didn't find any of it. They did find all the weapons. They also found various articles of our clothing they wanted. The police took anything they thought was at all nice or worth money, mostly shoes and jackets.

The policemen held their noses as they searched us and our packs. We thought that was strange; we smelled fine to each other. One of the men mentioned that he thought the police smelled bad, speculating that maybe we smelled bad to them and they smelled bad to us because we were from different places. People from different parts of the world look different, so it made sense to us that people smell different as well.

Policemen involved in the bus incident pointed to particular members of our group while speaking loudly to each other in Nepali. They made fighting motions as they talked. It looked like they were explaining what each person in my group had done to them. Several officers beat the men who had done most of the fighting, stomping on them with their military boots and punching them in the face while holding on to their hair. We hated to see that but could do nothing about it. The beaten men were in very rough shape the next day.

It was getting dark by the time the police were done with the search and beatings. We would have to spend the night in jail. Dinner was rice and lentils with a few oranges to share. When any of us needed to use the bathroom that night, we had to be escorted by police. I was the last person in my group to ask to go. I really didn't want to pee there, but I thought I'd reached the point when I couldn't hold it any longer. When I got up to go to the bathroom, I asked one of the men in my group to come with me for protection. An officer shook his head at the man and beckoned me toward him with his finger. He looked at me with a sort of mischievous expression.

One of the men who was making his second attempt had been in a group with three women on his first crossing. When they were caught shortly after reaching Nepal, the women were all raped. Each woman was raped by every single one of the police officers who had caught them. The women hadn't even been able to walk the next day. The man told me that I should go ahead and pee right there on the floor of the holding room. He said that after all we'd already been through together, dealing with my pee on the floor for one night wasn't an issue. The other men in the group quickly agreed. Though I appreciated their support, I couldn't bring myself to go to the bathroom in front of all the men in my group and the police who were guarding us. I held my pee all night. I couldn't sleep from holding my pee. The police finally let me go with men from my group in the morning.

That morning, the police told our guide that they had talked to the Tibetan government about us. Their plan was to take us to a certain place where someone from the Tibetan government would pick us up. Even though we didn't trust them, we didn't have many options, so we reluctantly agreed. In the early afternoon, they walked us to the plaza of a large building a short distance from the police station. We were escorted by many police officers, some of them following close behind us with their rifles aimed in our direction. The plaza was closed off to the street by a tall iron gate. They brought us inside the gate and told us to sit down and wait.

This time, there really was a representative of the Tibetan government ready to meet us. A woman from the Tibetan government ransomed us from the police for three thousand Nepalese rupees per person, about twelve U.S. dollars. She welcomed us and said she was glad we were safe, then took some basic information from all of us, writing our names and ages down in a notebook. I could tell she was friendly right away, even though I couldn't understand what she was saying until the guide translated her words. She spoke in the Lhasa dialect, which was used as the common language for the refugee community in India. It felt like she had come and saved our lives.

17. My First Taste of Freedom

AFTER THE WOMAN finished taking down our information, she put us on a bus to a refugee center in the city, where we were given food and a room to stay in. Monks and nuns like me received new robes because we had all crossed over in street clothes. It felt amazing to finally be through to safety. There were around seven hundred refugees at the center in all, far more than the center was designed for. There were not enough beds for everyone, and they had difficulty managing the crowd in the cafeteria.

We were processed at the center the next day. Officials wrote down our names, our parents' names, our ages, and where we were from, then started making documents for us. They also started the paperwork for sending us to our next destinations. Monks were given the choice of going to a monastery or attending the Tibetan Transit School in Dharamsala, India. There was no monastery space available at the time for nuns. When I heard I would have to go to the school instead of to a monastery, I told them they were crazy. I had zero interest in going to school. I was a nun and belonged in a monastery. I didn't want to be at a mixed-gender school with people going around doing whatever boys and girls do. The officials tried to reassure me by saying I could go to the school first and look for a monastery while I was there. I wasn't happy about it but did agree to go to the school, thinking I would be able to work it out when I got to India.

The food at the refugee center, though decent, could not satisfy our insatiable hunger. We never felt full after a meal. Anytime we ate, we felt hungry again as soon as the food ran out. Most of the little money we had left went toward buying extra food in the city, and we still wanted more. I'd order bowls of thukpa, and wonder where it all went after I quickly finished it. Coming out of an experience of not having enough to eat, anytime we saw food it felt like we better be sure to eat it while we had the chance.

For meals at the refugee center, they brought out huge piles of food and had us all line up for it. People starting lining up more than an hour before each meal. We were so eager to get the food that we'd push each other in line. Sometimes people got pushed out of the line altogether. They would try to squeeze back in, and if they couldn't, they had to go back to the end of the line. With so many hungry people competing to eat first, a typical day in the cafeteria was just short of a fight.

The main thing that prevented us from actually fighting was one man, Lobsang Norbu, who worked for the refugee center. Lobsang Norbu went around the line trying to keep us in order. Although not a particularly big guy, he could be intimidating when angry. He didn't hesitate to grab unruly people by the shirt and send them to the back of the line. When the situation started to get really out of control, he'd get a brick from the yard to threaten us with.

While at the refugee center I met a woman from my village who was living in Kathmandu. Her first marriage in Tibet had been a love marriage against the wishes of both their parents. It was a famous love story in the area. Unfortunately her husband was killed in a tractor accident. He had ignored a warning from her about an unfavorable dream she had the night before he died. After he died she nearly went crazy. She found it too painful to stay in the same village where they had lived together and left for India. Leaving her young son with her husband's family, she crossed over the mountains. The young boy used to talk about the day he was going to grow up and ride the family's donkey to India to see her.

She occasionally came by the refugee center to ask if there were any new arrivals from near our village, and when she heard I was there, she invited me to come visit. She didn't recognize me at first. When I told her my name, she knew who I was, and she was happy to see me. She was very eager to hear all the news from home. There were no phones in our village at the time, so it was a rare chance for her to hear about her family. The first thing she asked about was her son. I told her about her son's plan to see her on a donkey, making her laugh and cry. She told me how much she missed her first husband and asked about each and every person in the village around her age.

A strange thing happened when I visited this woman. She went downstairs to a small restaurant below her apartment to pick up some tea after showing me to her door, and I went inside alone. At the exact moment I put one foot through her door, I felt an uncontrollable urge to pee. I hadn't needed to go before that at all, then once my foot went through the doorway, my need to pee was unbearable. I froze where I was halfway into her apartment. If I'd held it for just a few minutes, the woman could have shown me to the shared bathroom in her building, but the urge was too strong. The pee came out straight down on the floor, missing my robes. That was a relief because it saved me from the embarrassment of explaining what happened. I pretended not to know anything when the woman came back and asked about the water on the floor. She cleaned it up with a mop and moved on.

This may have been one of the most significant events in my life. In Tibetan culture, widows are supposed to take special measures to purify their homes before monks or nuns visit to avoid causing a certain type of spiritual pollution. Strange as it may sound, peeing is sometimes considered a sign of pollution. Some people say that monks who don't keep their vows are likely to wet themselves during assemblies. The issue of widows isn't something I believed in that much myself, but something did seem to change in my life after that day. The sense of protection or good fortune I'd had went away.

Years later, I went to a lama to talk about my life and my future, and what he said reminded me of that day. I was no longer a nun at the time, and this lama had no way to know I ever had been, yet he stated early in our conversation that I used to be under special spiritual protection. He said that a few years earlier, I had been as well guarded by spiritual beings as a queen is by the king. That ended, the lama told me, when I encountered spiritual pollution through contact with a widow, someone with unusually strong negative energy. According to the lama, I was abandoned by the spiritual beings that previously protected me after I came into contact with this person. He said I would meet the right husband one day, not very soon, and would then see gradual improvement over time, like climbing up stairs one by one, eventually leading to a happy life. Until then, I would have bad luck and difficulty accomplishing even simple plans.

I'm not sure what to think myself. What the lama said sounded true, but I've never taken the issue of pollution from widows as seriously as some other people, and this woman only showed me kindness. She was friendly and helpful to me, so I don't want to think she caused a problem for me or blame her for anything bad that happened in my life. I appreciate that she treated me well, and even if it is true that she interfered with my spiritual protection, I can't be angry with her. She certainly never intended for anything to happen.

We stayed at the refugee center in Kathmandu for one month. After one month in Kathmandu, we were sent to Delhi. Delhi was a whole new experience for me. We hadn't seen anything like Delhi's hectic crowds and congestion where we stayed in Kathmandu. I was amazed to watch people as they crossed the street. People had to walk pretty much right through the busy moving traffic. The refugee center there wasn't so overcrowded, and we didn't have to wait in a long line for meals.

18. Dharamsala at Last

From Delhi I went on to my final destination: Dharamsala, India. Dharamsala is the seat of the Tibetan government in exile, the residence of the Dalai Lama, and the location of the Tibetan Transit School. About ten of us from my group would be staying at the school, and the monks from the group would be stopping in Dharamsala before moving on to monasteries in southern India or nearby Bir village. When I reached Dharamsala, my long period of travel was finally over. More importantly, I was close to realizing the goal of my journey: seeing the Dalai Lama.

We arrived in the McLeod Ganj area of Dharamsala on an overnight bus from Delhi. We stayed a week at the refugee center there, essentially a large open room with mattresses set out on the floor and a smaller separate room for women. Breakfast was ready for us when we arrived. While waiting in line for food, I heard someone with a familiar accent hawking Tibetan bread in the hallway.

McLeod Ganj is a small enough place that it is easy to quickly connect with other Tibetans from each region. The bread seller was from the same region as me and had already heard the news about a nun from Amdo coming to town. He took me to his apartment, where he told me all about Dharamsala and my cousin living a short bus ride away in Norbulingka. He said my cousin was expecting to see me soon. I stayed at his apartment overnight before coming back to the refugee center.

His apartment was a preview of what I could expect for myself eventually. In Tibet, we always had a large stock of food in storage and used huge pans to cook for our large family. This apartment was small, and everything in it was to scale with the room. Instead of a storage room filled with food, there was only enough to use day by day, and a small burner tucked in the corner took the place of a kitchen. Looking around the apartment made me feel hungry.

The next morning at the refugee center, workers went over our information again. After processing we each received a piece of paper granting access to see the Dalai Lama. The slips of paper were good for any time the Dalai Lama was in Dharamsala and had time available for an audience with refugees. There wasn't a set schedule for when that happened, so some people left Dharamsala soon after they arrived, holding on to their slips of paper for later.

Any time the Dalai Lama arrives in Dharamsala, there are sure to be refugees waiting to see him. I can imagine how busy he must be. He travels all over the world teaching about Buddhism and the Tibetan situation, then has a lot of work to do whenever he comes back to Dharamsala. In America, the president is done by the end of eight years, but the Dalai Lama has been Tibet's spiritual leader for his entire life.

I was happy to wait at the refugee center until I had a chance for an audience. As it turned out, I didn't have to wait long. After only six days, we were told the Dalai Lama would be available to see us the next day. That was great news to hear. I already had adequate nun's robes; everyone else went out to buy the nicest chubas they could afford so they could wear them in front of the Dalai Lama.

The audience the Dalai Lama held with us was a genuine dream come true. Everyone in Tibet dreams of seeing the Dalai Lama, and for us it really happened. It was more than worth everything I'd been through to get to India. The emotions we felt in the presence of the Dalai Lama after coming so far and through so much suffering on the way were too powerful to try to express in words. All of us cried throughout the audience out of joy and sadness. It didn't matter that I couldn't understand his words in Lhasa dialect. It was amazing simply to be in his presence.

When the audience was over we had to face the reality of new lives ahead of us in a foreign land far away from our families. Refugees under age thirty were able start our lives in India at the Tibetan Transit School. The Tibetan government in exile sponsors the school and all the services it provides. We received free meals, healthcare, soap, a toothbrush and toothpaste, and a small allowance for personal expenses. Most importantly, the school gave us stability while we settled in to our new lives. I can't imagine what I would have done without the school. Some Western charities also help fund the school. I wish I could thank all the people who helped; their donations really did make a big difference for us students.

The school was still fairly new when I went there, with an unfinished campus built with temporary materials. Students before us had done much of the construction themselves. Most of the buildings were made of concrete and corrugated metal. These materials offered little refuge from the cold of winter, and they only intensified the summer heat. During the rainy season, teachers struggled to be heard over the beat of heavy rain on the metal roofs.

Graduates of the school used to tell us how lucky we were to have the concrete and metal. It hadn't been long since the students lived in tents that sometimes blew down into the river. Work on improving conditions continued during my time there, though at a somewhat slower pace. Students before us had worked every day. We worked only on the weekends, mostly moving dirt and rocks to clear space for new and better buildings.

A couple hundred women shared no more than five bathrooms and a few showers. The bathrooms were a serious problem through the rainy season, when the river water we used for everything gave us all stomach problems. After classes everyone ran to the bathrooms. None of us wanted to be stuck at the end of the line with stomach problems. Men's and women's spaces at the school, including bathrooms, were kept absolutely separate; women could not use the men's bathrooms even if there were no line. Men can pee just about anywhere in India, so the men usually had a much shorter bathroom wait. In place of showers, men and women both could go down to the river to rinse off and wash hair while wearing shorts or light pants. Women always went in groups to avoid trouble from local men who sometimes snuck around behind the rocks to watch us.

We lived twenty people per room, sleeping in bunk beds pushed together so close our knees almost touched our neighbors. The beds got horrible bedbug infestations each summer. As soon as the lights went off, the bugs came out, making us scratch and turn all night. In the morning we could see blood on our white sheets from all the bugs we'd smashed in our sleep. Attempts by the school to exterminate the bugs were fruitless. Our only defense was to tuck our pants into our socks and fold our shirt collars tight up against our necks to keep too many of them from getting inside our clothes. I slept near the light and often gave in to the temptation to turn on the light during the night to scare the bugs off my bed. Once the light went on we could see the bugs scurrying away. No one ever complained about me turning the lights on; I don't think any of us were getting much sleep anyway. Some of the boys tried to escape the bugs by sleeping on the roof, until the school administrators found out and stopped that for fear they might get up during the night and fall off.

Strict order was maintained in the school at all times. Students who broke school rules were typically punished by being assigned to work in the kitchen for a day. Work in the kitchen started at six o'clock in the morning and lasted the entire day. The school had a rotation set up for all the students to help in the kitchen, which was put off by a day whenever there were rule breakers to do the work. It was usually boys who got in trouble, and the women loved it when they did. There were a few boys in particular who got caught smoking or sleeping in on a regular basis. Thanks to them, the rest of us got nice long breaks between our shifts in the kitchen.

All the students participated in an hour-long prayer to Dolma (the female bodhisattva of compassion also known as Tara) every day. It was a nice part of the day for me. I was happy to be part of a large group practicing our religion, and the prayers gave me a peaceful feeling. For most of the year the prayer sessions were held in the afternoon following morning classes and lunch. In the summer the sessions were held early in the morning after an assembly, making up for a three-hour break during the heat of midday. A lot of us had a hard time getting up so early, at four or five in the morning, especially when we'd been fighting bedbugs all night. When it was time to get up, the student leader in each room blew a whistle, and we all had to be present in the assembly hall ten minutes later. Once the assembly started, student leaders went around to check for anyone still in bed.

The first thing we did each morning at the assembly was sing the Tibetan national anthem and other songs about Tibet. Singing our national anthem always made me proud. My favorite song was one with lyrics encouraging Tibetans from all three regions to come together to work for freedom. Even though I'm a terrible singer, I loved singing about freedom for Tibet with my classmates at the assemblies.

Unity of the three regions was an important theme at the school. Many foreigners may think of Tibet as the "Tibetan Autonomous Region" province of China, when in reality Tibet is much bigger, more than double the size of the T.A.R. Tibet has three regions: Lhasa (also known as U-Tsang), Amdo, and Kham. All three regions are bound together by certain shared cultural characteristics and reverence for the Dalai Lama, and all three also have their own unique features.

Lhasa is the seat of the Dalai Lamas and the historical Tibetan government. Tibetans from Lhasa are supposed to be the smartest, as well as sometimes clever in a negative way. My region, Amdo, is the birthplace of the present Dalai Lama and the location of several important monasteries. The critical view of Amdo is that it is the region most heavily influenced by Chinese culture, most notably in cooking. Kham is classically Tibetan, a land populated mainly by nomadic herders.

Students from each region tended to socialize primarily with other students from their own area. Fights occasionally broke out between students from the different regions. When fights happened, authorities at the school told us very strongly that Tibetans cannot be fighting among ourselves. The school taught us that it is very important for Tibetans to come together if we are going to save our shared culture.

Another area of division that our community needed to work on was between the new arrivals and the Indian-born Tibetan community. Wealthier and more worldly than us, many Indian-born Tibetans looked down on our rough habits and difficulty managing simple things like taking a bus. We did look ridiculous sometimes. We struggled with life in India, and some of the habits we learned on our farms or tending animals looked odd; like the Tibetan men who, used to yelling to each other over long distances while tending animals, still yelled when they were right next to someone. When Indian-born Tibetans wanted to make fun of us, they'd say they could tell we were new by looking at our toes. We were supposed to have extra big toes from working outside without shoes.

That kind of talk hurt our feelings and made us resent the Indian-born community. We'd dismiss them by saying they'd lost their own culture and were no longer real Tibetans like us. Whatever our differences though, the school was right that we all have to come together.

There is no way our small community can fight for freedom unless we are a united community.

After the patriotic songs were over, we'd hear a speech from the principal, then all the students who had gotten in some kind of trouble were called up to the front of the assembly. Sometimes there were four or five people in trouble, and they'd try to hide behind each other. When the principal saw that, he made sure each person was separated enough to be clearly seen. Tibetan girls are supposed to be shy, causing extra embarrassment when a girl was called up. The boys made it worse by whistling at the girls. Fortunately that never happened to me. I did occasionally fall asleep at the summer assemblies, but I was never caught. Before falling asleep I would put a prayer book on my lap and rest my head on my hand in such a way that it looked like I was studying the book.

The most memorable assembly was the time the principal had to explain how to use the bathrooms at the school. In Tibet our habit was to go outdoors and use smooth rocks to clean with. The school had typical Indian–style bathrooms with squat toilets, a faucet, and a pitcher of water. Some of the students had been bringing rocks into the bathroom and tossing the rocks in the toilet when they were done. The rocks clogged up the toilets, and the cleaners were tired of taking them out. To resolve the problem, the principal had to stand in front of us all and show us exactly what to do with the faucet and pitcher. Everyone had a big laugh.

Academics at the school focused on language studies and Tibetan history. Learning about Tibetan history was enjoyable and exciting for me. Language study was not. While the three regions of Tibet share a common alphabet and grammar, pronunciation of the let-ters varies between regions and each region has its own vocabulary. The Lhasa dialect spoken in India was entirely new to me. I had to learn to communicate in the Lhasa dialect at the same time that I was studying English and Hindi. Back home I'd already had to learn some Chinese. I was feeling fed up with languages. My least favorite class was English because I couldn't think of any likely scenario in which I'd have to use it. Unlike other refugees hoping to obtain visas to English-speaking countries, I saw my future in a monastery.

As much as I deeply appreciated the school and all the assistance I received, I felt miserable there. I didn't think it was where I belonged. Before I'd come to India, I had been sure I would find a monastery. For some reason, although there were numerous monasteries for monks in India, monasteries for nuns were very limited. It was a major disappointment that I couldn't find one with space for me. There were about eight other nuns at the school with the same problem. If it had been easy to go back to Tibet, I was definitely ready to go home a short time after I'd arrived at the school.

I badly missed my home and my family. The school was near a river that students sometimes came down to for quiet when they needed to study; I used to come down to the river to have a place where I could cry and yell from the sadness of missing home. I often thought about sleeping next to my mother, which I did until I was fifteen and went to the monastery. That time with my mother was a good part of my life; if I could, I'd still like to sleep with my mother every night.

I missed my favorite foods too. The school always served rice and lentils for lunch, and I kept waiting for the one day we'd get thukpa. For a long time, I would ask another nun what we were getting for lunch every day until she finally told me to stop asking. She said I could safely assume that, from now on, lunch would always be rice and lentils. She had already been there for over a year before I arrived. I couldn't imagine that she could go on for that long eating rice and lentils every day. The whole situation at the school seemed impossible deal with for so long.

After a year I started to adjust and get used to living in India, but I still wanted to go home. I had a strong desire to live as a nun in a

Losar morning at the Tibetan Transit School. I'm the nun
on the right, with the friend who told me to expect
rice and lentils for lunch every day.

monastery, and I never stopped missing my family. While most of the
other students quickly spent their allowance from the school, I kept
almost all of mine for my return home. I saved up a modest amount
of money for a bus ticket and food, then waited to find someone else
who was also thinking of going back. I wanted to have someone I
knew and trusted with me before trying to cross over again.

Saving up money for a return trip to Tibet wasn't easy. Our hundred rupees had to cover anything not provided by the school such
as shampoo, underwear, and warm clothes for winter. The biggest
luxury I could afford was to, on rare special occasions, buy two fried
eggs for ten rupees at the chai stall across the street from the school.
There was not always enough money left over for women to buy tam-
pons. We layered pieces of scrap fabric, which we washed and reused.

While I was waiting to find a companion to cross back into Tibet
with me, I started receiving unwanted attention from one of my

classmates. I had originally met him at the refugee center in Nepal. We'd connected there because he was from a city not very far from my village. We'd bonded over our common home and shared experiences since meeting in Nepal, and we became close friends. One day he started telling me that he was interested in having sex with a nun. I understood he was talking about me and told him he shouldn't talk to me like that. I let him know that I planned to be a nun my whole life and had no interest in sex or marriage, so he needed to stop. I also explained to him that Buddhist teachings say that anyone who forces another person to have sex will definitely have a terrible rebirth. He continued to mention his interest in having sex with a nun to me frequently anyway, saying he didn't care about his next life. He said he only cared about what he wanted right now and didn't think his rebirth was anyone else's business.

One morning in the summer I accidentally encountered him after morning prayers. I had gone up to the third floor of one of the school buildings looking for a quiet place to study before classes started. I expected to find it empty because it was under construction. This boy happened to already be there studying. When he saw me come in, he came up to me and said that this was our big chance. I tried to excuse myself, telling him I hadn't expected to find anyone there and would look for someplace else to study. Before I could leave, he pushed me into a dark corner. As he was grabbing me, I told him I would yell out for the school security if he tried to do anything. He, and maybe both of us, would be kicked out of the school if I did yell, but I couldn't let this happen. He pulled down my pajama pants and unzipped his own pants. We struggled over my pants, me trying to pull them up and him pulling them back down. As we struggled, he pushed himself against me, and I could feel his penis touch me. I yelled, and he stopped.

He hadn't succeeded in forcing full sex with me; however, what happened wasn't okay for a nun. It wasn't clear to me whether I could remain a nun after that experience, and I didn't have a relationship with a lama I was comfortable asking. I was too embarrassed to ask just any lama or knowledgeable monk. In my situation, I do think I might have been allowed to stay a nun, but I didn't feel like one anymore. A nun is supposed to be ritually clean and spiritual; I felt dirty. For a week I pretended to be too sick to go to classes while I thought about what to do. After thinking about it, I decided I didn't feel I could be a nun anymore, and I gave up my robes.

I don't know how this person could have done that to me. We had both been through a lot of difficulty. Since meeting in Nepal, we had been through a lot of that difficulty together. For just a small thing, he ruined my life as a nun. He hadn't even gotten what he wanted while doing great damage to me. Giving up my robes left me completely adrift. I had planned on being a nun my entire life, and now I had no plan at all. There was nothing else I was interested in doing with my life, and I had no idea how I was going to live on my own in India when I left school. I felt like an abandoned child. I didn't know how I would get food to eat or where I would sleep.

Not long after that experience I came into another similar situation. I was visiting a friend who had quit school to work at a restaurant with her boyfriend. The owner had left the restaurant early, and the place was closed for the night. The boyfriend was living at the restaurant and made us some food there. After dinner he and his friend showed us a pornographic movie. I wasn't comfortable with that and started saying it was late and my friend and I should leave.

The men said it was okay if I wasn't comfortable with the movie and turned it off. They started making tea and invited us to stay a little longer. My friend got up, I assumed to use the bathroom, and was gone a long time. When I went to check on her, I found her in the hallway kissing her boyfriend. I came back to the room with the other man and told him it was time for me to leave. He grabbed my purse and wouldn't let me go. He was trying to touch me and kiss me. I told him to go away and asked him who the hell he thought he

On my bunk at the Tibetan Transit School after giving up my nun's robes.

was doing that. He responded by telling me how much better than me he was, saying he had more money and education than me and that I should be glad to get a chance with a man like him. He let me know it was ridiculous for me to think that I was too good for him.

I got very angry about that. I fought with him to get away, and then he grabbed me and pushed me into the bedroom. He took off each piece of my clothing. I was screaming, crying, and begging him to let me go. My friend and her boyfriend came in, and when they saw what he was doing, they just stood there. They didn't do anything to try to help. After he took off all my clothes, I tried to hide under the blanket, only to have him yank it from me. He took away all my clothes and hid them from me. He said that no matter how much I cried and yelled, I couldn't have them back until morning. I had to spend the entire night naked, sharing the bed with my friend and the two men. When it was time to sleep, at least he put the blanket back on the bed.

I was absolutely, unbelievably angry and frustrated all night. I could have killed him if I had a gun. I feel like this kind of person is worse than any animal, worse than a wolf. A wolf only kills other animals because it's hungry. It doesn't understand the other animal's feelings or make it cry and beg. There are some people in the world who don't care about other people's feelings no matter how much they cry and beg. The man who raped me, the man who sexually assaulted me, and this person were all like that. They could understand that my crying and begging meant that they were doing something awful to me, and they didn't care. This person who took off my clothes lives in Belgium now. Years later I saw him on Skype while he was visiting another Tibetan I know there. He tried to apologize and make nice with me, but it didn't change what he did.

Not all the young Tibetan men in Dharamsala are a problem, but those who do make trouble are highly visible. They give the entire Tibetan community in India a bad reputation and make life difficult for Tibetan women. I don't really think all these bad things that happened to me mean that Tibetan men are especially bad; it means that people need good government or somewhere to complain when there are problems, or else bad people know they can get away with crazy behavior.

I was fortunate to have the school to provide me with some stability over that difficult time. The school had recently extended its original three-year course of languages and Tibetan history to include an additional year of study in a locally employable trade. Former students had been having difficulty supporting themselves when they left the school, so the school had added the extra period of job skill training. Choices for trade skills included thanka painting, tailoring, and continuing study of English.

I chose to be a tailor. Now that I was no longer a nun, I had to think about how I would survive in India. I knew that there was a need for tailoring in the local Tibetan community, and I thought that was my best option. Unlike in my English classes, I was a good student in tailoring, and it worked out well for me as a job when school was over.

19. Life on My Own

AFTER FOUR YEARS at the Tibetan Transit School, it was time to move on. Up until then the school's sponsorship had been essential to my life. The thought that I would have to go out and take care of myself was intimidating. I knew that supporting myself in India would be difficult and, if I failed, I could find myself in desperate circumstances.

The fortunes of graduates from the school varied. The luckiest ones received personal sponsorships from foreign tourists they met in McLeod Ganj. It's possible to have a reasonably comfortable life in India for very little money, making even modest ongoing donations from abroad go a long way. Some young men managed to live very comfortably from the sponsorships they arranged from serial relationships with foreign women.

Many graduates fell on hard times after leaving the school. India is not an easy place for a refugee. Unemployment is a problem for everyone, and there are no safety nets to fall into. Some former students had to sleep in the woods and visit friends during the day for food. We all need a plan to stay alive. For some it was a job in India, for others a visa to the West. For quite a few refugees the only workable plan was to return to China. Refugees who returned to China usually hoped to find a job using their English skills, such as working in tourism.

I was personally fortunate to have a cousin teaching at the Nor-bulingka Institute in Norbulingka, India, I could live with. The Nor-bulingka Institute is like a university for Tibetan culture. My cousin had been a respected geshe before giving up his monk's robes so he could earn money to support family members. He was well edu-cated, cared about people, and was a well-liked honest person. His behavior didn't change very much after he left his monastery.

My cousin treated me very well, like his own sister. I could tell he cared about me. It was a nice feeling to have someone like that in my life. I found some work as a tailor while I was there, enough to increase my savings and confidence. I ended up staying with him for about six months before moving back to Dharamsala.

My decision to leave was largely prompted by my cousin's attempt to arrange a marriage for me with one of his friends. The friend was wealthier and more successful than almost any other refugee in the area. He was rich enough to own a car, an unattainable luxury for most people around McLeod Ganj. This person told my cousin he was interested in me and asked him to introduce us. My cousin happily agreed to make the introduction. He thought it was import-ant for me to get married to secure a good future, and he knew I wouldn't have to worry about money if I married his friend. A lot of people are hungry in India, but this man had everything I could want. The man and my cousin both thought the match was more than good enough for me. They were so sure I would agree to the marriage that they never asked me what I thought.

My cousin sent me to a party at his friend's house. Not many other refugees had their own house. When I got to the party, some other guests were already there drinking and having a good time. Not long after I arrived, my cousin's friend announced in front of everyone that we were going to get engaged. It was a complete surprise to me and left me unsure what to do.

It was getting late, and he told me I was welcome to stay the night at his house with some of the other people from the party. I just wanted to get out of there. I should have explained to him that I wasn't interested in marrying him, but it's hard to look someone in the face and say that. Instead I excused myself to go use the bathroom. I had to turn down his effort to direct me toward his indoor Western-style bathroom by saying I preferred to go in the woods. I went outside and walked straight to the house of a woman I knew in the area. I slept at her house that night, then went back to my cousin's in the morning. He didn't exactly scold me, but his friend had called and told him what happened. After that, it was a little uncomfortable to stay at my cousin's place.

The part of Dharamsala I moved to after leaving my cousin's place is called "upper Dharamsala," or McLeod Ganj. A former hill station used by the British to escape summer heat on the plains, upper Dharamsala is separated from the main part of the city by a short climb up a mountain. The main part of Dharamsala is a typical medium-sized Indian city that easily absorbs the Tibetan presence there. In McLeod Ganj, however, Tibetan immigration has transformed the small mountain outpost. The complex with the temple and residence of the Dalai Lama is one of the main features of the town. Tibetans constitute a large part of McLeod Ganj's population, and the Dalai Lama's residence there attracts a seasonal swell of foreigners interested in Tibetan culture. The foreign tourists in turn attract Indian merchants to the area, primarily Kashmiris.

There are only two main roads through McLeod Ganj: Temple Road and Jogibara Road. Both originate at the bus stop on top of the road from lower Dharamsala. The bus stop is the hub of all traffic coming and going from McLeod Ganj as well as the location of several of the town's biggest businesses and a popular hangout. A third road originating at the bus stop leads up to the small village of Bhagsu, and the village of Dharamkot is a short hike away. The entire town is easily accessible on foot. The main part of Dharamsala can also be accessed on foot, though it is easier and quicker to take one of the taxis that run between McLeod Ganj and lower Dharamsala.

Temple Road was nicely paved, courtesy of donations by Richard Gere. Richard Gere also sponsored the town's only trash removal service. I was vaguely aware that Richard Gere was in American movies while I lived there, though locally he was mainly known for being friendly with the Dalai Lama and for sponsoring projects in the area. I heard a funny story about a Tibetan man working as a cleaner in a hotel Richard Gere had just left. The cleaner was surprised by a white woman who rushed into the room, yelling at him to leave everything exactly as Richard Gere left it. She jumped on the bed and rolled around on the sheets for a while. The Tibetan cleaner thought that was the strangest thing he'd ever seen.

Living on my own in McLeod Ganj got started as well as I could hope. I supported myself working as a tailor primarily by filling orders for traditional Tibetan items such as chubas. I worked out of my room, getting most of my business through word of mouth in the local Tibetan community. I wasn't getting rich, but I made enough to afford everything I needed for a simple life. There was one Tibetan man who helped me get many of my orders. We had been classmates at the Tibetan Transit School. We used to sit next to each other in class, and when I'd start to fall asleep during lessons, he was the one who always woke me up. He had encouraged my move to McLeod Ganj by telling me he could help me get started in business there.

I knew in advance that he was romantically interested in me. One weekend during school, I ran into him while I was out shopping in Dharamsala with a friend. When he asked me what I was doing, I'd told him I was thinking about buying a blanket except the one I liked was very expensive. He replied that he would be willing to buy the blanket for me, on the condition that we share it when we finished school. He was a shy person, and though he hadn't said it directly, I knew that he was asking if I would marry him. I told him I'd changed my mind and didn't need the blanket after all.

After I moved, he started to seriously ask me to marry him, and I still said no. If I had been looking for marriage at that time, maybe he would have been a good match for me. There were not many other men in Dharamsala who were financially stable like him, and his behavior was better than a lot of other men. However, I wasn't interested in him, or any man. Until I met the right person, I didn't have any interest in men or finding a husband.

20. Fiasco at the Disco

NOT LONG AFTER moving to McLeod Ganj, I became very interested in dance parties. It was a completely out-of-character change for me. Until that time I'd always stayed away from parties. The school had put on dances for the students once a month, and they were very popular. While all the other women from my room were always eager to go, I would only stay a short time. Nothing about dances appealed to me at all until I moved to McLeod Ganj. For some reason, about a month or so after I got there I changed my attitude and started to go out dancing all the time.

The one place for dance parties in McLeod Ganj was called the Rock 'n' Roll Disco. It was a single room in the upper level of a building at the bus stop, with a small non-alcoholic bar and a deejay. The music was heavy on the latest Bollywood hits and Michael Jackson. Men had to pay one hundred rupees to get in; women got in free.

One night at the Rock 'n' Roll Disco, I saw two foreigners. Although foreign tourists were nothing new in McLeod Ganj, it was the first time I'd seen white people at the Rock 'n' Roll. There was a man and a woman, and I assumed they were together. At first, I danced with my friends and didn't pay much attention to the foreign couple. A little later that night, the woman left without the man. I looked at him and noticed that he was looking back at me. I was curious about him mostly because I was curious about foreigners in general. Although I thought he was good looking, I wasn't thinking about pursuing a romantic relationship with a white man at that time. We danced near each other, close enough to bump into each other by mistake. I apologized, but it was too loud to talk much.

I came to the dance party that night with a male friend who was also from Amdo. He wasn't a boyfriend at all, only someone I knew and was friends with mainly because we came from the same place. We had been dancing separately the entire night since we'd arrived, but when he saw me dancing next to the white man, he came straight over and got between us. He clearly wasn't going to let us dance near each other. I told him "okay fine," and he went back to another part of the disco. As soon as he went off, the white man and I got close together again, and my friend came straight back between us. I could see he was getting angry, so I didn't dance with the foreign stranger for the rest of the night.

I stayed outside talking with friends gathered at the bus stop after the dance let out. The white man saw me and came over. He said hello, introduced himself, and asked me my name. His name was Evan. Before I could answer, I was interrupted by my friend once again. My friend was clearly upset, angrily telling Evan to leave me alone. He told Evan that you white people only come to India to visit a short time and to sleep with women. He was very angry and approaching Evan in an aggressive manner, almost certainly looking for a fight.

Evan had come to the dance with two Kashmiri friends. One of his friends, Ashik, jumped into the situation. A large and rough–looking man, Ashik got up close to my friend to tell him in clear terms to go back to Tibet. It was a tense moment, one that looked like it could deteriorate. Both my friend and Ashik appeared ready to fight. If it came that, the situation could have escalated out of control.

Tibetans and Kashmiris had an existing history of hostility in

McLeod Ganj. Tibetans have a share in the blame for that animosity, bringing prejudices against Muslims from back home with us to India. In parts of Tibet, Muslims and Tibetans compete for resources and are divided by language and culture. During the seasonal gathering of a valuable fungus used in Chinese medicine, land-use conflicts between Tibetans and Muslims can lead to violence.

On the Kashmiri side, jealousy and resentment toward the Tibetan community is common. Kashmiris in Dharamsala tend to identify as refugees of a sort themselves, caught in the middle of a border conflict between rival foreign occupiers. They chafe at the adoration shown to Tibetans by the same white visitors who are rude to them. Seeing the minority of Tibetan men who are frequently in the company of new foreign lovers or sponsors, some Kashmiris assume that Tibetans come to India just to exploit foreign sympathy. As one Dharamsala Kashmiri told Evan, "We hold our hands out to God alone; Tibetans hold their hands out to everyone."

Both the Tibetan and Kashmiri communities are protective of their own members. An injury to either one of them would have been seen as an affront to the entire community. If a fight between Ashik and my friend had evolved into something bigger, there could have been serious consequences.

As level-headed as Ashik was hot-tempered, Showket, the other Kashmiri with Evan, intervened. Showket put his arm over Evan's shoulder and calmly led him away. Embarrassed and nervous about what was going on, I left too. When my friend saw that I was leaving in the same direction as Evan and Showket, he chose to follow me rather than stay and fight.

All of us were staying in rooms on Jogibara Road. Headed to our separate destinations, we made a single procession along the narrow road. Evan and Showket were in the lead, followed by a female friend and me, and then my angry friend bringing up the rear.

My angry friend followed my woman friend and me up to my

room. He had been yelling at Evan all the way down the street and continued yelling until he got to my room. He made sure we went inside and told us not to go out again that night. Ironically, he made a point of telling us not to make trouble. I wish that there had been someone focused on protecting me like that when I'd needed it. In this situation, he was only making me embarrassed and feel bad for Evan. I thought Evan must be confused about what the hell was going on. I didn't know much about foreigners, but I was pretty sure my friend's behavior would look strange to someone who wasn't from Tibet.

I felt awful about what had happened. My friend had yelled all kinds of bad things in English to Evan. I decided I should try to find Evan the next morning to apologize. I felt better after that decision and went to sleep.

I had recognized Ashik. He had a small shop near my building and used to say hi to me when I passed by. Most of the shops in McLeod Ganj were open, facing the street, and when business was slow, the shopkeepers often chatted with whoever was going by. Sometimes passersby gathered in the shops to smoke cigarettes, drink chai, and play chess. Ashik was particularly keen on chatting with women. His shop was on the way to my building, and he frequently tried to engage me in conversation. Despite the fact I wanted nothing to do with Ashik, he was the only person I knew who could lead me to Evan, so I went to his shop first thing in the morning. Usually Ashik smiled when he saw me. That morning, he looked surprised. I told him I was sorry about the scene from the previous night, and Ashik responded by pointing out that my friend was crazy and almost caused a lot of trouble. I asked Ashik if he knew where to find Evan, and he took me to Evan's room nearby.

Evan had only just gotten up when we came to his door. He was surprised to see me too. Although he looked a little uncomfortable at first, he invited me in and made tea for us. When I told him I was sorry about the night before, he said it was okay and I didn't need to apologize. That was my first time using English with a foreigner. I never even tried to use English much in school, but we seemed to be able to communicate smoothly.

After tea in Evan's room, we went to my room for breakfast. A friend had recently shown me how to make a quick and easy bread using flour, sugar, eggs, and baking powder, and I decided to make it for Evan. When Evan saw what I was making, he said, "Wow, pancakes!" I had no idea it was a foreign food, but I was glad Evan liked it. I didn't know anything about maple syrup or forks, so we ate it plain, pulling off pieces like Indian chapati bread.

When we finished breakfast, I invited him to come to lower Dharamsala with me for tea before I caught a bus to Norbulingka. Losar was coming in a few days, and I was going to spend the holiday with my cousin. We went to the bus stop together to catch one of the special taxis that run between upper and lower Dharamsala. The taxis run on an unpredictable schedule, waiting at the bus stop until they have crammed in as many passengers as possible, often ten or more. Passengers are crammed in so tight that even the driver is squeezed as he speeds around the twisty mountain road. The taxi drivers are famous for encouraging women to sit next to them. They turn the steering wheel with their whole arm, sending their elbows up against the women's breasts. Before I learned how to drive, I thought that was the right way to steer a car. Now I can see what they were up to.

In lower Dharamsala we looked around the market, then went to a quiet restaurant for tea. My cousin's rich friend, the one who'd wanted to marry me, had taken me to a restaurant in the back of a nice hotel in Dharamsala once for lunch. I remembered it being a nice quiet place secluded from the city's chaotic traffic, unlike typical chai stalls with seating overflowing into the street. I decided to take Evan there because it was a good place for us to talk without a lot of noise and distraction, and because I didn't want other Tibetans to see us together.

We had tea and talked about America, where he was from, and his impressions of India. I was curious what foreigners were like and what they thought. I asked him whether white people were ever embarrassed. I'd heard of white people in McLeod Ganj kissing in the street, and at the time I thought if they weren't embarrassed about that, there might not be anything they could be embarrassed about. I suspected maybe even if white people were caught walking around with no pants, they'd still think, "So what?" I was a little surprised when Evan said that of course white people could be embarrassed.

I learned that Evan was volunteer teaching at the Multi Education Centre, better known as the Bob School after the name of the head teacher. The Multi Education Centre provided instruction in English at several different levels. While Bob was spending time back home in England, Evan and another American were in charge of the classes. The school was on vacation for Losar, and Bob would be coming back after the break. When Bob got back, Evan was planning to spend less time at the school and focus on seeing other parts of India before he went home.

After tea it was time for me to catch my bus to Norbulingka. I told Evan maybe we could see each other sometime after the holiday when I came back to McLeod Ganj. He thought that sounded like a good idea.

Several days passed before I came back to McLeod Ganj. I guess Evan couldn't wait to see me, because he came looking for me while I was gone. He left a written message with my neighbor across the hall. As soon I saw the message, I knew it was from Evan. It said he'd come by and he hoped to see me when I got back. He'd moved to a different room, and he left complicated directions that I didn't totally understand.

Unclear how to find Evan's new room, I went back to Ashik's shop, and Evan was already there. We talked that day, and soon we were seeing each other often. It felt comfortable when we were together.

We were from different worlds and spoke different languages, yet it was always easy for us to be around each other. Even if Evan was going to leave India and never see me again, I didn't think I'd regret the time I spent with him.

Many of the other white people that came through McLeod Ganj appeared to be insane. It looked like some of them were seriously trying their best to dress as crazily as possible. These foreigners wore clothes with strange designs and strong colors mixed together. Some men wore what appeared to be women's clothes. A lot of the foreigners with crazy clothes had crazy hair too. The few local Tibetans who had been to Western countries said that Westerners only dressed like that in India. I didn't think that made sense; I thought crazy clothes and crazy hair must be normal in the West. Evan wore simple clothes not much different than what Tibetan and Indian people wore. A friend of mine who noticed us spending time together remarked on several occasions how striking it was that Evan looked like a normal person.

He also looked poor. Some of his clothes were worse than what regular local people wore. He had one sweater in particular that was very worn out and had quarter-sized holes in it. Tibetans and Indians never wore old clothes unless they had to. When Tibetan people had any money, they liked to have nice clothes to show it. Other Tibetans with some small experience with foreigners claimed foreign students without much money came to India during school breaks because it was much cheaper to live there; I guessed that was what was happening with Evan.

Evan's living circumstances added to my perception of his poverty. When I went to visit him in his new room, I noticed that he didn't have the right pans or utensils to use with the small, borrowed burner he cooked with. I watched him cook rice in a pan and burn it on the bottom, and I could tell cooking in these circumstances wasn't coming easily to him. A regular meal at most restaurants didn't cost much, usually less than one American dollar. He must not have enough money to go to even a cheap restaurant, I thought, or else he wouldn't be going through all this difficulty to cook in his room.

He was having just as much trouble with his laundry. I asked him if he needed help with his laundry after seeing dirty clothes all over the room, but he insisted no, he had it under control. The next time I saw him, he was doing the laundry himself. I found him with one of his pants legs rolled up, stirring a tub of laundry with his foot. To actually get clothes clean it's necessary to really scrub them by hand. The water in the bucket becomes thick with the dirt, then the tub has to be emptied and refilled. The whole process should be repeated until the water stays clean during the scrubbing. Hiring a dhobi wallah (laundry worker) to do it in the river isn't expensive. I asked Evan who did his laundry in America and didn't have a clue what he was talking about when he said he used a washing machine.

Feeling sorry for him, I invited Evan to eat dinner at my place. I did want to spend time with him, but I invited him mostly because I thought he needed my help to get good food and save money, and it was just as easy for me to cook for two as for myself. I made vegetable thukpa, and he asked for seconds. Since he liked it, I told him he could come have lunch or dinner with me every day if he wanted. I thought it must have been difficult for him to be so poor in a foreign country, and I felt like I was doing him a big favor making sure he got enough to eat.

After we'd been spending time with each other about a month, Evan's friend Manzoor invited him to visit Kashmir, where his family lived. When Evan told me about his plan to go to Kashmir for ten days, my first thought was that it was too far away and expensive for him to travel there. I didn't want him to go anyway; I wanted him to stay where I was. Knowing Evan wanted to see more of India than just McLeod Ganj, I didn't say anything.

The morning he was getting ready to go, I realized for the first time that I had deep feelings for him. It was hard for me to let him go anywhere. This trip felt like a rehearsal for the day when he would return to America. I struggled to hold back my tears as he and Manzoor prepared to leave. Evan sensed my feelings and asked if I would like to come with them. I was pretty sure Evan would pay for me, but that wasn't made totally clear. Although I did want to go with them, I said no because I couldn't afford to spend any money on travel and I was worried that it would be difficult for Evan to pay for me even if he was planning to.

I started to feel bored and lonely in McLeod Ganj while Evan was gone. My friends were still there, but it didn't feel right to me. Seeing the places we spent time together made me miss him even more, so I decided to go to Norbulingka to stay with my cousin until Evan came back. At the end of ten days, I received a call in Norbulingka from my friend Lhamo. Lhamo had seen Evan looking for me at my apartment. I came back to McLeod Ganj right away, threw my stuff in my room, and went out to find Evan.

Evan's room was locked when I got there. I checked at Manzoor's hotel and was told Evan had recently left. Next I went to Showket's shop to ask if he'd seen Evan. Evan and a few other foreigners often left messages for each other with Showket about where they were going or what their plans were. Showket told me Evan and Kate, the white woman I'd seen him with at the Rock 'n' Roll Disco, were decorating Easter eggs in Kate's room. When I arrived at Kate's room, Evan quickly came out to meet me in front of the door. I gave him a big hug and kiss, drawing the attention of a few local men hanging around the area. I was so happy to see him I couldn't help myself.

Knowing that Evan's trip to India would soon be coming to an end with our future still very uncertain was difficult for me. It was hard for me to think about. I already wasn't sure I would ever see my family again, and now it looked like I was going to lose another person I cared about. I didn't exactly think I was going to marry

Evan, but I also didn't want to give up our relationship. It was hard for me to picture myself finding another man I could trust like Evan.

I had to keep my relationship with Evan secret from other Tibetans. It was considered bad for a Tibetan woman to be with a white man. When other Tibetans saw us together, I always told them Evan was just a friend. Evan's Kashmiri friends all knew about us, as did a few other foreigners in McLeod Ganj, but I couldn't be honest about our relationship with even my closest Tibetan friends. McLeod Ganj is a small place, one where everyone knows everyone else and news spreads quickly. I couldn't completely trust anyone to keep a scandal like my relationship with Evan secret. Evan also kept our relationship hidden from the Tibetans he knew. If anyone was on to us, they didn't say anything.

Another reason I had to keep our relationship secret was that men from my region might be jealous. I don't think I'm that special, but there were not many other women from Amdo in the refugee community. Most new refugees are young men, and that is especially true for areas like mine that are farther from India. Given the number of young men from my region unsuccessfully looking for a girlfriend, they might not have been happy that someone from America had taken one of the few available Amdo women.

21. Evan Returns to America

EVENTUALLY the time came when Evan had to return to America. In an uncharacteristically romantic gesture, he gave me a thoughtful going–away present. He had traded his hiking boots to Ashik for a wooden box with intricate hand–carved decorations. It was a Kashmiri "magic box" that could only be unlocked by sliding a secret panel. Inside the box, he put a necklace from Showket's shop he'd seen me admiring in the past, a piece of amber he'd been given before his trip to India for its positive energy, a miniature Buddha statue in the Indian style, and a cassette recording of James Brown's greatest hits. I listened to that cassette endless times after he left. I couldn't tell what most of the songs were about beyond "So good! So good!," but I enjoyed listening to it to remember Evan.

A few days before Evan left McLeod Ganj, I went to Delhi ahead of him to check on the progress of my application for a Tibetan passport. Refugees born in India are considered citizens of Tibet and receive their documentation through the government in exile. Those of us born in Tibet all have birth certificates stating we were born in India, or we would have to get all our documentation through China. The passports were good for ten years, so like many refugees, I had applied for one to be prepared if I wanted to travel in the future. It was a good thing I did. The timeframe for receiving one was very long in the best–case scenario.

I had applied for my passport about a year before, the usual time it took to process an application. It was a good time for me to go to Delhi to pick up the passport and get a chance to say goodbye to Evan at the same time. It turned out my passport was not ready, but I was still happy to have the opportunity to spend some final time with Evan. We had ten days together in Majnu ka Tilla, Delhi's Tibetan colony, before his flight left.

I was waiting for Evan when he got off the bus. I'd already found a room in the center of the colony for us to stay in, a room memorable for its abundance of mosquitoes. Majnu ka Tilla is located on the banks of the Jamuna River, the breeding ground, it seemed, of all the mosquitoes in India. Mosquitoes gathered on the ceiling at night, waiting for the lights to go out to descend on us. The ceiling would look almost as though it had been painted black with mosquitoes. After flicking off the light switch each night, we'd hurry under the blankets, leaving an opening just big enough to let us breathe. Because Buddhists believe all life is precious, I was reluctant to use poisonous spray on them. I could have put up with them for ten days; Evan could not. After two or three nights of mosquito attacks, I agreed to borrow insect spray to clear them off the ceiling before bed. I tried to save a few by catching them and putting them out the door while Evan went after them with the spray. It looked like rain as the spray went to work.

As the date for Evan's departure home drew nearer, he asked me what I wanted to do with my future. I told him my first wish was to go back to Tibet to be with my family, and if that weren't possible, my second wish was to go to a Western country to make money to help my family. We talked for a long time about the risks of going back to Tibet and about my prospects for a life in the West. We already had a good idea of how hard it would be for me to get a visa. We'd looked at the possibility of a student or tourist visa and concluded they weren't realistic options. A woman from England, Heather, had tried to help me get an au pair visa to Europe, also without success.

With Evan at Raj Ghat in Delhi.

Given the difficulty of obtaining visas legitimately, we talked about buying a visa on the black market. Visas to any Western country could be bought for a range of prices depending on demand and the risk involved in producing them. Black market visas were exactly the same as other visas in every way except that the people receiving them didn't go through an application process.

Buying visas was the only way for most Tibetans to emigrate to the West. They weren't cheap. The price of a visa was far beyond the means of regular Tibetan or Indian people, and it's not easy to borrow a large amount of money from a friend when planning to leave the country. The usual place to borrow the money was from monasteries. Monasteries typically have funds and Tibetans are unlikely to cheat monks. After arriving in the West, people sent the majority of their earnings back to the monastery for the first several years. During those years, many Tibetans worked at Chinese restaurants for below minimum wage. One man I know saved money by spending nights sleeping on a row of chairs in the restaurant where he worked.

At the time Evan and I were in Majnu ka Tilla discussing our plans for the future, visas to America were going for the equivalent of about fifteen thousand American dollars. To me, that was an unbelievable amount of money. It might as well have been fifteen million dollars as far as I was concerned. When Evan suggested he might be able to help me buy a visa, I realized at last he wasn't as poor as I thought. I was actually a little angry that I'd been feeding him all this time, thinking he was completely broke, when in fact he had access to fifteen thousand dollars all along.

For the time being, we decided that I would look into the possibility of buying a visa. We would keep in touch, investigate our options, and see how we felt about the situation over time. I could tell from our conversations that Evan did want me to come to America and that he also had some reservations. He warned me that I might be disappointed by the Western world and have trouble adapting. I understood what he was saying, but I didn't have a lot of better choices. I wanted to be with Evan, there wasn't much for me in India, and it was difficult to get back home to Tibet.

A friend and I accompanied Evan to the airport on his last day. We all walked to the airport gate together. Before he left, I gave Evan a last kiss on the cheek and said, "Please don't forget me." My friend later told me how embarrassed he was to see that display of affection. He said a crowd of people had been looking at us. It was very sad for me to watch Evan go. I was also jealous. All he had to do to go home was take an airplane. For me, getting home was almost impossible and could only be done by risking my life.

I got up the next morning feeling miserable and empty. Everything around me felt different. Memories of times I'd spent with Evan followed me everywhere I went. Evan had always been completely honest and straightforward with me in every conversation. I realized that I'd found it easy to share all my feelings with someone like that. When you share your deep feelings with a person you love, your love also becomes a deep love. I already missed Evan so much I couldn't wait to see him. At the same time, it seemed impossible to get a visa. I talked to several people I thought might know about visas, always getting a vague answers about what to do.

I went to the Tibetan passport office to find out when my passport would be ready, only to be told that it was stuck at the Indian office that verifies and approves Tibetan passports. I gave a man working in the office five hundred rupees (about eleven dollars at the time) in the hope of fixing the problem. He put the money inside a folded piece of paper with my name and his phone number on it and gave it to someone higher up in the office. When I came back a few days later, I was told someone had come by to verify my residence when I wasn't home, and the passport application had been inactive ever since. That's all I got for my five hundred rupees. I had to give them another fifteen hundred rupees to restart work on my application.

In India, these demands for payments to perform simple government functions are typical. Government workers receive little official salary, making their real living mainly from bribes. The bureaucracy in India is designed to facilitate that. It is not only a matter of spending money to get out of a long wait or complicated procedure; simple procedures require signatures from specific office holders. You must get that person's signature, and there is no recourse if he or she refuses.

If a person wants to get around the law, bribes can buy any document and fix any problem. The downside is that bribes are just as necessary to obtain every document and fix every problem for a person trying to follow the law as someone trying to break it. In my case, even though there was no reason for the office to have my passport incomplete after more than a year, paying the fifteen-hundred-rupee bribe was the only way I could restart the process.

Evan sent emails to me almost every day while I waited for my passport. They were nice to get, although reading and writing English was much harder for me than speaking. I understood the emails he sent pretty well; sending my own was a little more difficult. I had to use a dictionary to find the spelling of almost every word. Phone calls were complicated because I did not have a phone to receive calls, and the international phone closest to me was only open during the day. I called Evan several times during what was the middle of the night for him before realizing that night and day in India and America are opposite. I would have been okay with waking Evan up except for the fact he was staying with his parents in Maine for three months between his return to America and starting graduate school. I thought I might give his parents a bad feeling toward me if I woke up everyone.

Evan was never romantic on the phone when I called him. He was not the kind of person who talked sweetly or expressed his emotions. There were times I told him I loved him or how much I missed him at the end of the call, and he just said, "Okay, bye." I hated when we got off the phone like that. I was missing him so much that at times I wished I'd never met him. I wondered if I might be making a mistake putting so much emotion into this relationship. I thought about how he had told me many times before leaving that there was a good chance we wouldn't see each other after he went back to America.

I've never thought of myself as attractive or as a good catch. As a kid my sister used to call me Onli-nu, "Donkey Face." She never used my real name, only Onli-nu. Nobody ever told me "Good job!" or said nice things about me. It seemed that I must have been kidding myself to think that Evan would still be interested in me after going back to America. I thought of myself as ugly, uneducated, and poor. I couldn't think of any good reason he would want to keep up his relationship with me. I started to think that I needed to hold back my feelings. I tried to wait longer between calls. I'd wait one day, maybe two days, but that was as long as I could go. After that, I would feel like I just had to call him.

I felt strongly that I needed to get to America to see Evan in person as soon as possible. I asked a Tibetan friend who knew someone in the passport office to try to help me get my application moving a little faster. When we went to the office, we were told that my passport was totally stuck. My friend and I had to go back and forth between this and another office for a number of days trying to sort out the problem. A man from Ladakh (a small and culturally Buddhist corner of India's Jammu and Kashmir province) working in one of the offices offered to do a favor for me only if I did a favor for him, meaning sex. Frustrated, I gave up at his office.

I was so discouraged I stopped trying for a few months. I hoped that maybe the office would work out the issues without a bribe. I didn't really expect that to happen, I just needed to get away from it for a while.

Months passed without any progress. It became clear I had to make a choice between giving up or putting everything I had into getting a visa. I decided I needed to focus on getting my passport. I moved in with a woman I knew for what would clearly be a long-term stay in Delhi. Her husband was in Belgium, and she was waiting for him to get refugee status and apply for a visa for her. My friend Lhamo from Dharamsala was also in Delhi at the time, shopping for a black-market visa to France.

One good thing that happened at that time was that I got a cellphone. My cousin's friend, a monk, was moving to a monastery in southern India. He didn't think he'd need a cellphone at the monastery, so he gave his to me. Evan could call me directly on my new phone. By this time he had moved out of his parents' house to start graduate school in Denver, and he started calling me almost every day. He was becoming more affectionate on the phone, which meant a lot to me.

One night I told Evan about news I'd heard involving people arrested for trying to buy visas. They lost their money and had to spend time in jail. He didn't want that to happen to me and offered a new suggestion. He said we try a fiancée visa. I had no idea what a fiancée was, but I told him it sounded like a good idea. He sent me an email with more details, and it was only then that I understood what he was talking about. Evan never went down on his knees and asked me to marry him; suggesting over the phone that we try a fiancée visa was about as close as we came to that. Evan filed the main part of the fiancée visa application in America, and before long, I received a notice for a date to come to the U.S. Embassy for a visa interview.

While my passport application process dragged on I started taking tailor orders in Delhi to support myself. Most of my work was making Tibetan religious designs on pillows that were sold in a nearby store. For sewing these designs on the pillows by hand, from first thing in the morning until dark, I could make one hundred rupees per day, or about two dollars. Each pillow sold at the store for more than twenty dollars.

Evan sent me money for an airplane ticket to America, anticipating I would soon get my passport and visa. He sent more than thirty thousand rupees. That was a lot of money for me. In India, it is not easy to make that much. Although I appreciated the money for the plane ticket, I felt that he should have sent more to show he cared about me. I knew Evan had a job at his school, and I'd heard people in America could make ten dollars an hour, compared to the two dollars a day I was making. Not knowing how expensive it is to live in America, I wasn't sure what he could be doing with all that money.

I decided I had no choice but to pay someone to fix the problems with my passport to make sure it was ready in time for me to interview for a visa. I took all my visa information to the Tibetan passport office to tell them how much time had passed and that I needed the passport soon. The person I talked to didn't have good news. He said my passport application couldn't be saved, and I would have to start over. I couldn't believe he said that. I'd already been waiting for well over a year; starting all over again sounded absurd. He insisted that it was my only chance, and I didn't know what else to do, so I paid the fees and started waiting again. To speed things up, I went to the office responsible for verifying my residence and paid a two–thousand–rupee bribe.

That money was well spent; the inquiry came after only one month. I took the two inquiry workers out to a restaurant and gave them each an additional five hundred rupees. The bribes helped my application get moving, but not fast enough. While my passport slowly moved forward, the time came for my visa interview, forcing me to go to the U.S. embassy to reschedule.

22. The Worst Thing I've Ever Done

WHILE I WAITED for my passport in Delhi, my roommate and I spent most of our time working on pillows together, and my roommate loved to gossip as we worked. She seemed to know everything that was going on in Majnu ka Tilla. According to her, my friend Lhamo and her roommate had been saying a lot of bad things about me, such as that I was in a relationship with a white man just for money and a visa. That made me upset for a number of reasons, especially so because Lhamo had been one of my best friends for a long time. When Lhamo had needed someone to provide a signature on some documents in order to get an abortion years earlier, she'd come to me. I had helped her, even though I felt guilty for being partially responsible for the abortion. It struck me as a terrible betrayal for her to be spreading rumors about me now.

My roommate wanted to get revenge on Lhamo and her roommate by putting up graffiti that said they were whores. My roommate couldn't do it herself because she couldn't write, not even her own name. What she was really saying was she wanted me to do it. Although I was upset about what she told me the women had done, I wouldn't agree to write the graffiti. Both women had husbands in other countries, and they each had a kid. I knew it would hurt their entire families if I wrote the graffiti my roommate wanted me to. When I refused to do that, my roommate came up with a second idea. Lhamo had borrowed a couple hundred thousand rupees to buy a visa to France, and my roommate wanted to steal it. I said no to that too, knowing that Lhamo was already in the process of buying the visa. If the money were gone when the visa was ready, she would lose the money and her chance to go to France, where her husband was.

My roommate was quiet for a few days, then she started up again. She told me more about things Lhamo and her roommate were saying, pressing me to do something about it. She argued that if we stole the money, we could give half to the poor. She said it would be good to punish the women for what they were doing and good to use the money to help poor people. Meanwhile my resentment toward Lhamo had been growing. Helping her get the abortion wasn't just any favor. Thinking about these two things, my anger toward Lhamo and the good the money could do for the poor, I agreed to help steal the money.

My roommate had formerly been friends with Lhamo's roommate, now her worst enemy, and had kept a spare key to their apartment. She planned the theft for a night when Lhamo and the other woman were both out attending a party. We were all in the same building, making it easy for us to see when Lhamo and her roommate weren't home. She gave me the key to the apartment and told me to go get the money while she watched the entrance of the building from the roof. Her job was to warn me if anyone were coming.

I took the key to the apartment. I felt very uncomfortable about what I was doing, even while I was on my way to do it. I knew if anyone did catch me stealing the money, it would be a huge embarrassment. The news would spread through the Tibetan community in India and go on to Tibetan exiles all over the world, perhaps eventually making its way back to my family. I felt more and more uneasy about the plan as I got closer to the room. In spite of the second thoughts in my mind all the way to the apartment, I didn't stop.

I got to the room. My hand was shaking so much as I opened the door that it was hard to get the key in the lock. I knew Lhamo kept the money in a suitcase. Inside the room, I found the suitcase and opened it. It was filled with bundles of rupees. I'd never seen so much money; it was a little intimidating to look at. I grabbed what I could carry in my hands, not checking how much it was, then got out of the apartment and locked it behind me. My roommate came in right behind me when I entered our room. When I threw the money on the bed, she said, "Oh my gosh, that's a lot of money." Seeing so much money laid out, she thought maybe we should just keep one bundle and put the rest back. I was already having big regrets and feeling awful about the situation. The last thing I wanted to do was go back to the apartment, but I did. Leaving behind one bundle of cash in our room, I ran back to Lhamo's apartment, returned the rest of the money, and quickly got out.

I later figured out that my roommate had her own reasons for stealing the money. She wanted to make Lhamo suspect her roommate of the theft. By making Lhamo suspect her roommate had stolen the money, she planned to set the two women against each other. My roommate was very clever at manipulating people and punishing anyone she was angry with like that.

She also needed money. She was a person who liked to enjoy life and have nice things, a lifestyle financed primarily with money from her husband in Belgium. Her husband usually sent her some money every month, but not always. He had a gambling problem and didn't always have any money to send her. When we stole the money from Lhamo, she had not received anything from him for several months.

The bundle of money we kept had fifty thousand rupees in it, of which we each took half. Only a few days after we stole the money, my roommate used the majority of her share to buy an expensive gold necklace. She barely had enough for living expenses and didn't know when more money would come, yet that was what she did with her half of the money. I was shocked she spent so much so quickly.

After she bought the necklace, it was apparent she wasn't going to follow through on her plan to give the money to the poor. Even with poverty surrounding us, I wasn't sure how I could distribute my half of the money to the poor on my own. Delhi didn't have any soup kitchens I knew of or organizations I could simply make a donation to. It wouldn't have been a good idea for me to distribute the money in handouts. It could have put me in danger, and at the very minimum I could be sure India's persistent beggars would follow me everywhere I went. Giving the money to any Tibetans wasn't possible since it would raise questions over where it came from. Unsure what to do with the money, I held on to it. I didn't give it to the poor, and I didn't use it for myself right away. Eventually I used it to pay for visa expenses.

Lhamo noticed the missing money after a few days. I heard about the discovery from my roommate, who had been offering Lhamo phony consolation. I started to feel very sorry for Lhamo. We had put her in a very bad situation. I felt very guilty and uncomfortable for making her life so difficult. I had done something that was much worse than the things she was accused of doing to me. I was also starting to have doubts about my roommate. I didn't trust her anymore, and I began to suspect that all the talk about Lhamo and her roommate spreading rumors about me wasn't really true.

My roommate's husband called from Belgium in the middle of the night a couple of days after she bought the necklace. The Tibetan community in Belgium is small, and news spreads quickly. The latest story spreading there was that my roommate stole Lhamo's money to buy her gold necklace. The good news for me was that nobody suspected my involvement. I felt awful anyway.

Lhamo did get her visa to France, but I was still angry with myself for what I'd done. I felt stupid for believing everything my roommate had told me. I felt like the kind of stupid person it was easy for anyone to take advantage of. The fact that I'd stolen from a friend made me feel worse. I knew it was bad to steal from anyone, and felt that stealing from a friend must make me worse than a regular thief. The more time passed, the more I regretted it. The part I regretted the most was that I didn't even need the money at the time. Evan had sent me more than thirty thousand rupees to buy a ticket if I got my visa, and I was sure he would send more if I asked for it.

My regrets made me more eager than ever to get to America. A lot of people had done bad things to me in India, and I had done something myself I knew was terrible. I felt like being around bad people was making me a bad person too. I wanted to get out of this place with these people. I believe that people tend to become like the people they spend time around. I wanted to be with Evan, who I knew to be an honest person and good man. I saw myself going in the wrong direction from being around the wrong kind of people, and I wanted to turn that around. I wanted to be a better person than I was when I stole the money.

I held on to my regret silently for a very long time. I finally decided to tell Evan about it years after we were married. Even though I was afraid of what he might think, I wanted the person I love to know who I really am. It wasn't easy, but it felt good to finally tell someone the truth. Although he was shocked I'd done what I'd done, he didn't judge me for it. After I told him, I did feel better, but I knew there was something else I needed to do. I still needed to fix the situation with Lhamo.

Around that same time we bought a computer, and soon I found Lhamo through the Internet. When we first met again on Skype, it was embarrassing to see her face to face after what I'd done. I told Evan I'd talked with Lhamo as soon as he walked in the door after work that day. I told him I was glad to have talked to her but still felt bad about taking her money. He advised me to tell Lhamo the truth, and suggested I offer to pay Lhamo back my share of what we took.

I was very glad to hear him say that. It was important for me to have that support before telling Lhamo what I'd done. As much as I needed to unburden myself of the weight of my secret, there were reasons to stay quiet. I was mostly worried that the news would get back to my family if Lhamo were angry and told other Tibetans what I'd done. Although I didn't care what anyone else thought about me, I didn't want my parents and siblings to find out. When I had earlier talked to my former roommate about telling Lhamo the truth and paying her back, she'd told me I definitely shouldn't say anything.

I was also glad that Evan had been the one to suggest paying back the money. I wasn't working at the time, and Evan did not make very much at his job working with children with developmental disabil-ities. We were living in a very miserly way, as we still do. We didn't spend money on anything unnecessary. We were very careful about spending just a little money on one piece of clothing at a thrift store and always used every bite of leftover food. Paying back Lhamo was a lot of money for us, and it was worth every penny. It was a big relief for me to give it back.

The second time I talked to Lhamo, I looked at her face, took a deep breath, and told her I knew who stole her money. She laughed at me and said, "Hey, what are you talking about?" I said again very seriously that I knew who stole the money. She looked at me sur-prised and said, "Really?" I told her I stole it, and she laughed at me again. It looked like she thought I was joking for sure. I felt so sorry for her and embarrassed about what I had done. I felt like I'd done the worst thing in the world. It was very difficult for me to go on with telling her the truth. I felt like telling her the truth about what I did was more difficult than it had been to cross the mountains into India. I started crying. When I started crying, she was quiet for a while; she could tell I wasn't joking.

After some thought, she said the past was in the past, and there was no need for me to cry. She said it had been a very difficult time for her and the theft had made her very sad, but now she was not in that situation anymore. I begged her to please forgive me and offered to pay back what I'd taken, more than that if she wanted. To my relief, she could see I was truly sorry and forgave me. She was glad I'd told her the truth and to finally know what really happened to the money.

Lhamo and I talked for a long time that night, going over the whole history of what had gone on. I found out that my former roommate had also been telling Lhamo I was saying bad things about her. She had turned us against each other for no reason. Learning that made me angry with my ex-roommate. She was about ten years older than me and had been acting like a teenager. Mostly though, I'm glad that Lhamo and I got our friendship back.

Lhamo wasn't insistent about repayment. I appreciated that, but it was important to me to repay her. I felt guiltier the longer I held on to the money, and the only way to change that was to repay my share of what we stole. It happened to be a particularly good time for Lhamo to get the money back. Her father was in the hospital in Tibet, and she needed money to pay for his treatment.

23. My Fiancée Visa Is Denied

FINALLY I RECEIVED good news about my passport: My second application was approved within four months. I was immediately anxious to go to my visa interview. I wanted to get away from people like my roommate and all the corrupt government office workers I had been dealing with. When I received a new interview date, I went feeling hopeful and optimistic.

I brought an interpreter with me because my English was not always perfectly clear, and some of the words related to the visa application were new to me. When my turn came to talk to a visa interviewer, the man on the other side of the window refused to let me use the interpreter. He wanted me to answer all the questions myself without any help. When my interpreter tried to explain his questions to me anyway, he cut her off with a sharp, "I'm talking to her!"

The interviewer had a thick Indian accent I was having trouble understanding, and my Tibetan accent was equally hard for him to understand. The more our communication got off track, the more nervous I got, causing me to make more mistakes. It didn't help that the interviewer was unfriendly and impatient. He was barking at me in quick sentences and interrupting my answers with new questions. Near the end, the interviewer said he couldn't understand how I could possibly communicate with Evan if I couldn't understand him (yelling at me in a thick accent).

At the end of the interview, he told me he would need a letter from Evan explaining how we communicated, and additional tax records from Evan's father, who was acting as my joint financial sponsor. The interview had been a stressful experience, but I thought the conclusion sounded positive. It looked like I needed to get the letter and tax records and then I could have my visa. I called Evan right away to tell him the things I needed. We were both starting to feel excited about the prospect of me being on my way to America before too long.

I received the letter and tax records four days after the interview. I went back to the embassy and gave them the new documents and my passport. Without hearing anyone say exactly whether my application would be approved, I got the idea I was definitely going to get a visa. I had brought the documents the interviewer asked for, and I interpreted the fact that they took my passport to indicate they were going to put a visa in it.

It took more than one month for the embassy to get back to me. After a month of waiting, I received a call from the embassy saying they were sending out my passport. I waited eagerly. The passport arrived in a big envelope, but inside my passport there was no visa. A piece of paper inside the envelope had a lot of words on it that were new to me. I brought it to someone who could help me read it. The letter said I was "unable to establish to the satisfaction of a consular officer that a credible relationship exists." "It appears that no bona fide relationship exists between the beneficiary and the petitioner," read the letter, "therefore, the petition is being returned to the NVC office for disposition."

I felt incredibly angry and frustrated. It had been extremely difficult and expensive for me to get the passport and difficult and expensive to apply for the visa. I had put up with a lot of trouble along the way, navigating the endlessly discouraging corruption of Indian bureaucracy on a daily basis. I had been living in Delhi, going through all this for over a year only for my passport and visa. The final insult was that the embassy had asked me to bring extra documents, taken my passport, then rejected my application anyway. I was overwhelmed by disappointment. I was holding a piece of paper that said my chance to get out of India, away from my roommate and people who had done bad things to me, was over. What's worse, I thought my relationship with Evan was over. We did have a real relationship, and we were serious about getting married. It was a bizarre and terrible feeling to be told by a piece of paper that an impatient man behind a plastic window had decided I hadn't provided adequate proof of our feelings for each other.

I didn't expect that there was any way for Evan to come to India again. My main reason to think that was because he was in school. In China, the rule is a person who leaves school is not allowed to ever come back. Evan had told me that he would be willing to come back to India if I needed him, and I'd always said no because I didn't want to create a problem in his life by making him leave school.

I called Evan with the bad news. I didn't have much to say; mostly I just cried into the phone. When I called, Evan was putting on a tuxedo in preparation for a friend's wedding. He was surprised, discouraged, and upset, but he couldn't talk long. He asked me to fax the paper to his father's office so he could read the rejection letter himself. Evan didn't have the fax number with him, so I had to call his parents' house to get the fax number from his mother. She couldn't understand my accent, which was especially hard to make out over the phone. It sounded to her like I was asking about a "sex number." She told me she was sorry, she didn't understand me, and I had better talk to Evan.

Evan cleared up the confusion with his mother when he arrived home. After reading the paper from the embassy, he called and told me not to worry. He said he would come to India to see me and we would figure out what to do next together. Even if it meant Evan would lose his chance to finish school, as I believed it would, it was the only way for us to be together. I told him to come as soon as possible. Thinking about Evan coming back made me feel better. Over a year had passed since we'd last seen each other in person, and America seemed so far away. I couldn't wait to see him again.

24. Evan Returns

EVAN WAS IN INDIA less than a week after reading the paper from the embassy. I was amazed at how quickly he was able to get a visa to India. He had been able to apply for his visa in the morning at the Indian consulate in New York and had taken a plane to India that night. It struck me as tremendously unfair that it was so fast and easy to go one way and so hard to go the other.

I got a room in a guesthouse in the Pahar Ganj section of Delhi for us. I didn't want Evan to meet my roommate, didn't want her to know what was going on in my life, and felt done with her all around. I hadn't said anything to her about my visa or Evan coming back to India. When she found out I was leaving the apartment in Majnu ka Tilla, she asked what my plans were. I told her I was going to Nepal.

Evan's plane arrived in Delhi at one or two in the morning. I got to the airport early to make sure I was there plenty of time before Evan arrived. I stood next to a railing overlooking the international arrivals terminal and the entrance ramp to the waiting area. There were people coming up the ramp all the time, and I had no idea when any particular flight was coming through. I watched each person who came up the ramp, being very careful to make sure I didn't miss Evan. I had to look carefully at each person because white people mostly look pretty similar to me. My neck started to hurt from being turned to my left side for so long.

After a long time waiting at the railing, my stomach began to hurt. It was probably the effect of the stress and excitement of what was going on. I had to go sit down. I hadn't been sitting very long, no more then ten minutes, when Evan came up the ramp. When I saw him, he was at the top of the ramp looking around the room for me. I couldn't believe I was seeing him. He had come all the way from America just for me. I ran over to Evan to give him a big hug and kiss. I didn't care that we were in the middle of a room full of people.

Within a couple of days we went to the embassy together with the hope of resolving the problems with my application for a fiancée visa. It was much easier with Evan there. I didn't need an interpreter, and we could go to the American Services desk to inquire about my visa application. It's not exactly what the American Services desk is for, but it was the only place we could talk to someone, and the embassy never picked up the phone when we called. The American we talked to first was very nice, but he wasn't able to help us understand what had happened with our visa. He had to ask an Indian.

The Indian employee declared the fiancée visa application was done and there was nothing we could do about that. Although he couldn't provide us with any explanation of why the application had been rejected, he did explain our options clearly. He recommended that we get married in India in order to apply for a spouse visa. With no hope of salvaging the fiancée visa, his advice made sense—the catch was that we would have to wait two months to apply. Evan had to stay in India for two months to be able to apply at the embassy in Delhi as a resident of India; otherwise he would have to go back to America and apply through the office with jurisdiction there.

We could get married any time while waiting. I asked the woman who had been my interpreter to help us. She took us to a certain lawyer she knew in a legal complex in Delhi, one with many tiny offices crammed in. Signs at the entrance to the complex warned visitors that cricket bats and hockey sticks were strictly forbidden. The lawyer strongly suggested we have a simple Indian wedding at a local temple. Evan and I were still fairly naïve about the expectations of the embassy and procedures in India, and we deferred to his judgment. In retrospect, it was a ridiculous idea we should never have agreed to.

As we later learned, marriage law in India is written with separate requirements depending on the religion of the people involved. Our situation was complicated by the fact that Evan was a Christian from America and I was a Buddhist from Tibet. Interreligious marriage was unusual in India and subject to a more complicated legal process. What we needed was a "special marriage" certificate, a document that takes time and work to get. This lawyer gave us advice that he most likely knew was unhelpful in order to get paid faster.

As a Tibetan Buddhist I was defined as a Hindu according to Indian marriage law. Evan was not. In order to get married in a local temple as the lawyer advised, it would not be enough for Evan to say, "Sure, I'm a Buddhist/Hindu," and get married to me. He had to officially convert to Hinduism, the reason why our wedding was performed at a temple run by the Arya Samaj, a Hindu supremacist organization that is one of the few faces of Hinduism that accepts converts. The lawyer brought a headdress and dress shirt for Evan, along with the conversion document and marriage certificate. We were confused from start to finish throughout the ceremony. Someone from the temple took photos for us to give the embassy. We never actually got those photos from the lawyer. I'm sure we looked every bit as confused as we really were and as silly as we felt.

After collecting our marriage document from the Hindu wedding, our plan was to pass time until we could apply for a spouse visa. Neither of us was eager to spend that time in Delhi. Delhi is scorching hot during the summer, and its unrelenting chaos is stressful to live with.

Pahar Ganj, where we were staying, felt like the very center of Delhi's heat and chaos. A popular destination for backpackers for its cheap lodging, as well as a busy market, the narrow streets of Pahar Ganj were packed with just about as much humanity as they could hold. From the first second we stepped out of our guesthouse, we were surrounded by raucous noise and commotion. During the regular blackouts, generators provided an inescapable din permeating the market.

Rather than remain in Pahar Ganj, we went back to the Dharamsala area to stay in the village of Dharamkot. Dharamkot is a quiet, peaceful place surrounded by forest and striking mountain views. The majority of tourists there are young Israelis coming off of their compulsory military service. In Dharamkot, they can relax in the peaceful environment and smoke hashish almost anywhere without being bothered by police. It's nothing unusual there to see people at restaurants smoking hashish through a chillium pipe while waiting for their orders.

It was the rainy season. The rain in Delhi had come in bursts of intense showers; in Dharamkot it was more of a constant drizzle. I didn't want to go down from the village into McLeod Ganj and get caught up in local drama, so I stayed behind at the guesthouse when Evan went to meet with old friends.

Evan's friend Manzoor was in McLeod Ganj and invited him to come back to Kashmir with him. Evan asked if I wanted to go, and I said yes. I wasn't interested in travel, but Evan had said good things about Kashmir, and we had to wait for two months anyway. Evan mentioned a few times on the way that the road between Jammu and Srinagar was an alarming experience. It was a twisting dirt road cut into the edge of Himalayan foothills, barely wide enough to accommodate two directions of traffic. Passing military trucks pushed all other vehicles almost to the very edge. For me it wasn't so bad. It was a lot like what I'd grown up with. In fact, many aspects of the beautiful scenery on the way reminded me of home.

Manzoor did not think the embassy would accept our Hindu marriage, and he was probably right. He advised us to get a secular court
marriage instead. He offered to look into finding someone to help us
get a secular marriage document while we were in Kashmir. In the
meantime, we could stay with his family until it was ready. At the
time, I didn't really understand what the difference was. I'd never
heard of anyone getting a document for marriage in Tibet, and I
thought the embassy would accept whatever we brought.

For a long time, we couldn't figure out why Manzoor's mother
Fatima was always closing the window in the room we stayed in. I
discovered the reason in a surprising way. Evan had amoebic dys-
entery, which he insisted for too long was only food poisoning, the
kind of thing foreigners in India get all the time. He became steadily
sicker, obviously suffering. On one occasion, right after he vomited
out the open window into a small grassy area between the house
and the wall around the property, I saw a massive snake slither past
his head. It was black with white spots and as thick as my leg. Evan's
head was resting on the sill, his eyes closed. I was afraid to speak
as I watched the huge snake slowly going by, just inches under his
head. I didn't want to attract the snake's attention by yelling out a
warning to him. After it was most of the way past, I finally yelled,
"SNAKE!" Evan looked up, surprised. I could still see its tail before
it disappeared, but Evan missed it completely. After that, we kept
the window closed. We checked the room every night before bed to
make sure there was no snake in the room with us. Even after we'd
done a thorough search, it was hard for me to relax. I couldn't stop
thinking about that huge snake. It was by far the biggest snake I've
ever seen.

Manzoor took his time looking for someone to help us arrange a
court marriage, and as the two months approached an end, we were
getting impatient. Very near the end of the two months, Manzoor
told us he had everything ready. He took us to a court complex,

where we met another man. We got there too late; the marriage office at that complex had closed early. We all got in a car and headed to a different office.

Events at the second office we went to were confusing. It was clearly a back-up plan. We had to pay a bribe to get a document there, but at least it was done that day. The other man Manzoor brought along definitely took a piece of the bribe we paid and asked for an additional payment after the document was complete. I was ready to get the money out of my purse, but Evan refused to pay. In the car on the way back, the man held our document hostage for the extra money he wanted. Evan demanded that he hand over the document without additional payment. A person I have not seen angry very often, Evan was furious in this situation. It was scary for me to see that; I thought for sure they were going to fight. The man got out of the car, taking the document with him. Again, I was ready to pay, but seeing Evan's anger, I put the money back in my purse. Evan started to get out of the car to follow the man, before Manzoor stopped him. Manzoor told Evan to stay there, and he would get the document. Manzoor got out and did get it.

We saw the man again later in the street back in Manzoor's neighborhood. He walked up to us to tell Evan he needed to pay the rest or "you and I will have a problem." We were planning to go to back to Delhi soon, so we just told him great, no problem, don't worry. Then, just ahead of the first day we were eligible to apply for the spouse visa in Delhi, we left Kashmir. We were still holding out hope that we could get the visa before the end of Evan's summer break, and we were hurrying as much as possible to make that happen.

We returned to Pahar Ganj, where we found lodging on a side road that was a little less crowded, offering an appreciable improvement over the constant noise and motion we'd been in before. We were feeling good, even a little optimistic. Now that Evan was there to talk with the embassy personnel and had demonstrated the authenticity of our relationship by coming all the way back to India for me, my visa seemed like a sure thing. We went to the embassy prepared with all of the paperwork for the spouse visa application, including the civil wedding document from Kashmir.

At the embassy we were escorted through a side door and past a small garden to a waiting room. There were several other couples in the room with us. Evan and I were one of the first couples to arrive and the last couple waiting. A polite woman finally came in to ask us to come with her to see a man in an office. The manager in the office, a local Indian, told us our document from Kashmir didn't meet the requirements of the embassy. He said we needed to get married under India's religion-based marriage laws, and then we could come back and reapply. He advised us to go to a legal complex in old Delhi to find a lawyer to guide us through the process. I can't be sure, but it looked like he might have been planning to get money from us. Too much of the time it seemed as if the job of lawyers in India is to transfer bribes to officials from people who need something from them.

Disappointed, we went to Delhi as he advised. It was a huge, busy, disorganized legal complex. We didn't make it far inside the gate before we were harangued by lawyers to use their services. We walked quickly through the initial crowd that converged around us, ignoring their yelled offers of legal assistance. A calm followed as we continued walking toward the main building. A young man lounging outside the main building approached us casually to ask what kind of help we needed in a much less pushy manner than the others, and we went with him. The lawyer this guy brought us to had a desk in a crowded area under a large awning in the back of the main building. The lawyer invited us to sit down and gave Evan his card. This lawyer advised us the easiest and fastest course of action was for us to get a Christian marriage. He knew a nearby church we could go to right away and have the wedding that very day. We negotiated the fee and agreed to the plan.

We took separate auto rickshaws to the church, the lawyer making sure we paid for his fare as well as our own. At the church the lawyer introduced us to the pastor who would be performing the wedding, then handed Evan some paperwork to fill in. As we waited for the lawyer to get someone to take photographs for the embassy, people started to filter into the church; I'm not sure why. It was my first time seeing the inside of a Christian church, and my overall impression was positive. I generally like religion, and this appeared to be a nice, peaceful place. When everything was ready, the pastor put on special robes and led the people that had come inside in some singing. When the singing was done, he performed a simple ceremony. I cried. We were really making promises to take each other as husband and wife and put rings bought back in Kashmir on each other's fingers. Unlike before when we'd only been interested in satisfying the embassy; this time I felt like we were really truly married.

It was sad at the same time, because we didn't have our families with us. The absence of my parents and family on my wedding day was a reminder that I was not in my own country. I thought about my sister's wedding day, when all the women in the village had come to send her off. I was around ten years old at the time. She'd ridden away to her husband's village on horseback, dressed in beautiful wedding clothes. While my mother cried watching her leave, I was thinking I couldn't wait for that to be me at the center of attention. It looked like such a wonderful day for her. On my own wedding day, I was torn between the joy of my future being married to someone I loved and the sadness of separation from my family.

We retrieved the photos of the wedding on a Sunday, and were in line at the embassy first thing Monday morning. As before, we were escorted to the waiting room for spouse applications, and as before, we were the last couple to be called. When we were called, we were brought back to see the manager in his office again. The manager gave us a certain reason why he wouldn't accept the Christian marriage in our case. I can't remember exactly what it was. I do remember it didn't make sense; it might have had something to do with me being from Tibet. Evan was clearly annoyed by the manager's explanation. He insisted on going to the American Services desk to complain. The friendly American at the desk deferred as usual to a local, who in this case appeared confused himself about what we had been told. He disappeared for a while to inquire into the situation. He came back with a photocopied page of Indian marriage law that supposedly justified the explanation we'd received from the manager. Evan wasn't at all convinced, but there was nowhere else to go to pursue the argument. The embassy worker told us to get a special marriage for people of different religions and walked away.

Frustrated and unsure what to do next, we returned to old Delhi, where we found the lawyer at his desk under the awning. We asked him to contact the embassy to resolve the problem with the Christian marriage, facilitate a special marriage, or return our money. He refused. He showed no sign of surprise nor offered any condolence. He blamed us for the problem. Putting on an air of great professional dignity, he advised that our only option was to get another marriage through him, for a new and higher fee.

That only made us more frustrated and fed up. I told him he was the kind of person who was like a wolf, and he was even starting to look like one. We argued at length with the lawyer, bringing considerable attention in our direction in that crowded compound. All this attention made the lawyer uncomfortable, prompting him to hurriedly walk away.

We stayed behind at his desk, determined to stay until we had some satisfactory resolution. He stayed away for a long time. I'm sure he expected us to go away eventually if he was gone long enough. As we waited by his desk, a number of people asked about our situation, and we told each of them exactly what was going on. Perhaps embarrassed by these conversations, the lawyer finally returned to request we come with him to see another lawyer he claimed could help. The second lawyer worked in an enclosed stall. This new lawyer asked what our problem was, and when we explained, said that of course our application had been rejected, that we needed to pay the embassy money. For a generous fee, she would make the arrangements.

There was no way we could trust either of them. We didn't know what to do; all we knew was we would never give more money to either of these two. We stayed in the office to argue about the money we'd already paid. The first lawyer eventually gave up the pretense that he had undertaken his work for us in good faith, claiming instead that he'd already spent the money. Next, he said the Christian pastor had it all. He gave us the pastor's phone number, telling us to call him about it. Before we went out to call the pastor, the lawyer asked for his card back.

We called the number. The pastor did not give a clear answer when Evan asked him if the lawyer were correct to say he had the money; he only told Evan to come down to the church, where he would explain everything we needed to know. We didn't need to go to the church; his equivocal answer was already everything we needed to know. We didn't have the will to go back and keep fighting with the lawyer. Depressed, we got in an auto rickshaw and went back to our guesthouse.

It was a terrible feeling to go back without any resolution or new hope. It felt like we were at a dead end. Evan and I didn't have any connections able to help us, and we didn't know how to navigate the system. Each time we asked anyone to help us, they only helped themselves by cheating us. We knew that corruption was standard; we did not know exactly when to pay bribes, and we didn't always know how to pay them. It felt like we were lost children. We didn't know which way to go or what we were supposed to do. We tried to keep going and were always hitting walls. There were people saying go this way, go that way, or follow me, and we couldn't believe any of them.

I was missing home terribly and feeling upset about the situation there. It was bad enough I was away from home; it made me feel worse that Tibetans don't even have freedom in our own country. I wished I'd been born somewhere I could go back to where people were honest and everything worked the way it's supposed to. Evan and I weren't doing anything wrong, just trying to get married, and it wasn't working for us. If I had been from somewhere with freedom, our marriage would have been easy.

Unsure what else to do, we went back to Delhi once again to look into getting a special marriage. This time, we walked through the main building hoping to find an office where special marriages were performed. We walked all around inside the building. It was largely empty, the complete opposite of the scene outside. People we asked for assistance didn't seem to know what we were talking about. Most professed ignorance or gave general suggestions of areas of the building that might have that type of office. After a long time going up and down stairs, poking our heads into offices, and asking everyone we saw for help, we finally received sound guidance: An old man told us we were in entirely the wrong place. He couldn't make out any reason at all why the embassy manager had told us to go there. He kindly wrote down the address of a marriage office about half an hour away for us before leaving.

The rickshaw dropped us off a short distance from the marriage office. As we approached the office, a lawyer saw where we were headed. The lawyer walked up to us, staying with us as we tried to walk away. He was talking as we walked, insisting there was no way to have a marriage done without a lawyer's help. As we passed a man getting on a motorcycle, the man looked at the lawyer following us and shook his head in our direction. He made a kind of sour face to let us know we didn't want the lawyer involved.

The lawyer stayed with us all the way to the marriage office. He talked over us while we tried to explain our situation to the office workers, until one of them finally made him go away. Two women worked in the office. One of the women proved herself to be the most honest and helpful government worker we encountered in India. This honest, helpful woman listened to what we were there for and told us exactly what we needed to do to prepare a packet of materials for a special marriage application.

Once the application was filled, it had to be signed by a particular official whose office was conveniently located next door. The honest woman told us clearly that we would have to pay something for the signature and gave us an idea of the upper limit of what we might agree to pay. She brought over a man who showed us to the office, where we received the signature we needed without any difficulty. Evan asked directly how much we needed to pay, a question the official brushed off by directing us to the man who brought us there. We didn't give him anything. I had originally thought there would be some complication and work involved, and then when all that happened was that the guy in the office next door, who was not even slightly busy, signed our document, I didn't want to pay for that. At that point we were very fed up with paying bribes and being taken advantage of. The go-between seemed mildly surprised we left him empty-handed, though not upset, giving the impression he had no personal interest either way.

Completed packet in hand, we were sent in to see the judge in charge of the marriage office the next morning. The judge greeted us with typical exaggerated airs of dignity. After looking over our packet, he pompously declared that it was both incomplete and incorrect, projecting offense that such an application would be brought before him. He called the honest woman into the room to criticize her for sending us in with this packet. Though the woman could not talk back to her superior, I could tell she was annoyed by his behavior.

If I had been comfortable doing the talking, I would have liked to give the judge some good advice. Here was a man who was clearly old, cranky, and unhappy. He needed to go home and get some rest; it was time for him to be preparing for his next life. I couldn't believe that he was still working in the office at his age, still thinking about cheating people this close to his death. When Tibetans get old, we focus on prayer and seeking forgiveness for our bad deeds. Tibetans want to make sure our actions in old age lead to a good rebirth. This judge was doing the complete opposite. He could see us almost crying, begging him for mercy, and he didn't have compassion even then. There's a good chance he's changed lives by now and is in a miserable realm or a hungry ghost. There's nothing money can buy worth that.

Evan drew the judge's attention to the fact that his objections were inconsistent with the instructions printed on the application form. The judge gestured toward the legal texts on his bookcase defiantly, declaring he could easily show the exact statutes he was referring to. When Evan asked him to do exactly that, the judge took down a book and firmly placed it on the desk in front of Evan. Evan found the section pertaining to marriage law, read it, then challenged the judge to explain his objections, to which the judge only laughed. Evidently amused by Evan's efforts, the judge changed his tone. He handed us the business card of a lawyer, saying we would need some help to complete our application correctly. This lawyer, he told us, was Tibetan and would understand our situation. Taking a more friendly approach now, the judge confided in us that with the lawyer's help, we wouldn't have to wait the usual month for the application to process. After handing us the Tibetan lawyer's card, he showed us the door.

I called the lawyer to set up a time to meet. We agreed to meet at the metro station in Connaught Place, then head to a restaurant to discuss our marriage application. Connaught Place was an upscale shopping area that inexplicably attracted tourists to pay the same prices at the same stores they found at home. We knew what the meeting with the lawyer was all about, and it wasn't completing our application correctly, but we didn't know what else to do. The Tibetan lawyer led us on a long walk to one of Connaught Place's high-end restaurants, where we all ordered tea at ten times the price charged anywhere else in India.

He started the conversation with new problems he'd identified in our application. Evan cut him short, asking him to focus on the objections raised by the judge. After a bit of awkward back and forth, the lawyer acknowledged that the judge's objections had no legal basis. However, he insisted, his new objections were valid and required his expert services. The conversation deteriorated from there. Evan was having a hard time accepting India's corruption. What the lawyer was saying didn't make sense, and that was making Evan crazy. The more Evan complained that he wasn't going to hire someone to bring up new objections, the more the lawyer smugly persisted in representing his actions as honorable defense of the law.

The lawyer eventually dropped his pretense of integrity only after it became clear the conversation was leading nowhere, finally laying out the fee the judge wanted to accept the application and the fee he wanted to make the deal. Both the fees were exorbitant. The lawyer wanted the equivalent of more than two hundred American dollars just to pass the bribe. I asked in Tibetan why he needed so much. He justified it by saying his fee was modest compared to what his fellow lawyers charge in America.

Evan and I went outside to discuss our choices. We were torn between desperation to get the marriage completed and disgust with the corrupt judge and his friend the greedy lawyer. We didn't want to give either of those jerks any money, yet we needed the judge to approve our application. The judge had sole jurisdiction over our place of residence. After talking it over, we decided that though we needed that particular judge, we didn't necessarily need that particular lawyer. We thought we could find any one of the many lawyers hanging around the marriage office to facilitate the bribe for less if this lawyer wouldn't agree to a steep discount.

We made the lawyer an offer that covered the judge's bribe with something extra for him. The extra we offered the lawyer was considerably less than what he was expecting, though it seemed generous to us in light of the fact he was doing virtually nothing to earn it. The way we saw it, turning down our offer, even at the lower amount, would be like turning down free money. He wanted the full amount or no deal. We told him no deal, and that was it. He got up and left without paying for his tea.

This Indian-born Tibetan lawyer was an even worse person than the corrupt Indians we had been dealing with. He could appreciate my situation in a way the Indians didn't. Rather than lift one finger to assist a fellow Tibetan, he'd only thought about his own profit. Tibetans like that are very shameless people. In the Tibetan community, there are heroes who have faced torture and sacrificed their own lives for our freedom, and then there are thieves like this lawyer.

Early the next morning, we went back to the area of the marriage office. As always, there were lawyers looking for work. We stopped one of them on the sidewalk to discuss our problem. We told him the size of the bribe we'd been told the judge was demanding and how much we were thinking of paying someone to deliver it. Given that the judge's office was within sight of this conversation, we asked the lawyer not to expect an excessive fee for taking a short walk to deliver the money. The lawyer was interested in our proposal, up to the part about the excessive fee. Urging us to consider the delicate nature of his work and the many efforts involved, he attempted to negotiate a higher rate. The same man who had earlier been our go-between for the signature we didn't pay for overheard the conversation. He had been drinking chai nearby as we talked with the lawyer. When his chai was done he walked over to us to give some advice. Before we paid anyone to handle a bribe, he said, we needed to talk to "Madam," referring to the honest woman at the marriage office.

The honest woman listened to our story of the events with the judge and the Tibetan lawyer with evident irritation. She took our complete and correct application packet to the office across from hers, which was dedicated to anticorruption affairs. This judge was soliciting bribes no more then ten feet from the anticorruption office. A woman in the anticorruption office conferred with the honest woman. They looked closely at our application, checking to make sure there were no genuine problems with it, and then both women went into the judge's office with our packet. When they came out, the honest woman told us that the judge had determined our application was correct and accepted it.

We went back to Pahar Ganj feeling triumphant. It was beyond our expectations for the marriage application to be accepted without a bribe. That elation was short lived. The phone rang; it was the honest woman from the marriage office calling to inform us the judge had raised a new objection based on one of the issues the Tibetan lawyer had dreamed up. At that time of day, it was too late to go back to the office to respond. There was nothing more we could do that day except try to take our minds off our problems watching American TV at the guesthouse.

We were back at the marriage office when it opened the next morning. We always came early for several reasons: to get stressful business out of the way, to take advantage of the cooler morning temperatures, and because there was no telling how long a task was going to take. Giving the judge a single document could take all day. If he came early and left, we would have to wait for him to come back, if he came back at all. Coming early guaranteed we caught him, but we had to wait for him to show up. When he did come, we had to wait for him to be ready to see us.

Late that morning, the judge arrived in a white government car with a driver. We stood up from the chairs in the entryway to his office as he walked inside, without receiving so much as a glance in our direction from the judge. Whatever he was doing in his office after arriving, it took a long time. We waited an hour or more before he let us in. He gave us the standard lecture when we entered his office, asserting that he was an important and busy person who didn't have time for us to be filing incomplete applications. For such a busy person, he took his time putting on a performance before taking our document. Once he did take it, he assured us our application was now complete.

We received another call after breakfast the next morning. The judge had a new objection requiring us to submit another new document. As before, it had to do with one of the issues the Tibetan lawyer had mentioned at the restaurant. We went back to the marriage office to supply the document, again waiting for hours to be let into his office to hand it to him. For a week or so, the morning calls requesting new documents or additional copies of previously submitted documents became part of our daily routine. Each time the honest woman called to inform us of the latest demand from the judge, her voice betrayed her growing embarrassment, and perhaps her own sense of helplessness. With each new demand, we certainly felt more helpless, and we also felt more determined to complete our application without giving the judge a bribe, even if that meant we had to spend our day waiting outside his office every day until he gave in. It didn't matter how long it took or how much aggravation we had to go through; we were not going to give this judge so much as a whiff of a paisa, the smallest denomination of Indian currency.

On the weekends we talked on the phone with Evan's parents. It was nice to have them to talk to about our ordeals, though I often wished we had good news from time to time. While talking with them about our issues with this judge, Evan's father asked if it were still possible to fix the situation with a bribe. It probably was, but neither of us would consider giving it. We hated that judge.

Despite every obstacle the judge put in front of us, we were always back waiting outside his office to see him every day without fail. For each new demand, the judge made sure we did plenty of waiting outside before he'd see us, and each time he saw us, he scolded us indignantly for our incomplete application. Eventually there came a point where he couldn't keep it up any longer. It's possible he ran out of imagination for new demands to place on us, or maybe our daily appearances were becoming an embarrassment for him. Whatever the reason was, the daily phone calls eventually stopped. Our application was accepted, and our photos were posted outside the office.

For special marriages, part of the standard process was for a paper with the names and photos of the bride and groom to be posted outside the marriage office for one month. As I understand it, that month was meant to give family members an opportunity to find out about plans for a special marriage between their son or daughter and a person of a different faith in time to put a stop to it. The problem with this system was that the papers with the names and photos of us and a few other couples planning special marriages were only visible to someone standing directly in front of the marriage office, on a remote side street. It was very unlikely that anyone who didn't work there would see the posted papers.

It took several days without receiving any more phone calls before we felt confident the judge was done creating problems. Delhi's heat kept us indoors under the fan for much of that time. Temperatures rising past 110 degrees made even short walks around the marketplace feel strenuous. Our preferred relief from the heat was to buy a lassi yogurt drink from a stall around the corner from our guesthouse. Sipping our lassis on the bench in front of the stall, we watched Pahar Ganj's busy population of backpackers, rickshaws, street hawkers, beggars, and cows pass us by. Some days, festive wedding parties or religious processions with decorative floats passed through the market. We would go out after sundown, and when we returned to the guesthouse, we would sit out on the balcony with peanuts or some other snack to watch the activity on the streets.

Once a convincing length of time passed without more objections from the judge, we were ready to leave Delhi. I'd heard the lake districts in the northern hills were beautiful, and much cooler, so we went to Nainital, an attractive small city around a lake ringed by mountains. We found a place to stay and settled in to spend the majority of our month of waiting for the marriage certificate there.

It rained steadily during our stay in Nainital, and once again, we found ourselves frequently trapped indoors. Evan and I were starting to get on each other's nerves from all this time together. Stress, frustration, and disappointment had become standard for us since Evan's return to India, and we were anxious about what would happen at the embassy with the special marriage. Being together in a small room for consecutive days of downpours without any outlet for our emotions other than each other proved to be a true test of our relationship, the kind of thing it would have been nice for the embassy to take into consideration.

During the occasional periods the rain let up, Nainital was a pleasant place to visit. There was a large and lively public space, a high-altitude zoo, and a Tibetan monastery within walking distance of town. We ran into a young Tibetan couple in Nainital I had known at the Tibetan Transit School. Their company was a welcome change, and I was especially glad to eat homemade Tibetan food at their apartment rather than getting each meal from small restaurants or street vendors. They were in town for business at a religious festival, selling women's shoes bought cheaply in Nepal.

The festival lasted a week, maybe two. The main event was the procession of a deity image on a float from a Hindu temple around the town, ending with immersion in the lake. The entire downtown was decorated for the event, its open space overrun by all types of vendors, rides, games, and amusements. Prime space was purchased by larger operations, but small sellers like my friends from the Tibetan Transit School could set up stands on the fringes of the festival. My friends had their shoes displayed on a simple Indian woven bed with a light wooden frame. Their sales were disappointing. As the festival slipped by, my friends first reduced their profit expectations, then sold shoes at cost, and finally sold some at a loss on the last day to unload their stock.

Seeing their meager living conditions, I felt sorry to watch their business struggle. Their situation is sadly typical of many Tibetan refugees in India. Jobs are scarce, and it's not easy to start a successful business. Without land to work or a family to turn to for support, the life of a refugee can be uncertain from day to day. That's why so many of the Tibetans in India go to great lengths to emigrate to the West, where they can expect a steady income.

As the end of our month–long wait drew closer, we left Nainital to return to Pahar Ganj. We nervously returned to the marriage office to check on our application. Everything was fine, and we set an appointment with the judge to complete the process. All that was left was for the judge to sign the marriage document in front of three witnesses. I gathered three Tibetans to act as witnesses, and we all appeared together at the marriage office on the morning of the appointed day. We arrived a little early to make sure everything was set. The honest woman greeted us and brought us to the waiting room on the side of the building.

We sat and talked and looked at magazines as time went by. A lot of time went by. We eventually went to see the honest woman to find out what was going on. She hadn't seen the judge yet, and she didn't have any way to contact him. It was getting to be well after lunchtime, and he was still missing and unreachable for our ten o'clock appointment.

Waiting for the judge with our three witnesses was a different sit-uation than the other times he'd made us wait for him. When it had only been the two of us, we didn't have to think about anyone else's plans or how long others' patience would hold out. Accustomed to American expectations, Evan was worried about our witnesses. For Tibetans, fortunately, it's more normal for people to do each other favors like that without complaint. As one of my friends told Evan, if we got the certificate that day at all, he would consider it fast for India.

The judge arrived a little after three o'clock. The honest woman stopped him on the way into his office to let him know we'd been there waiting all day. Unconcerned, he walked past us without apol-ogy or acknowledgment. He attended to some other business in his office before letting us in to finish the marriage. It was now past four. I have no doubt his lateness was intentional to punish us for failing to pay him a bribe. Finally he let us in and completed the marriage. It had been such a long day, and we were still uncertain about the reaction the embassy would have, so we didn't do anything special to celebrate that night.

25. A Final Push

IT WAS A HUGE RELIEF when the embassy accepted our special marriage. Even the security guard who had escorted us to the marriage waiting room for the third time was glad to hear the good news. It was still too early to relax though. Acceptance of our application was only one step of the visa process. Next, we had to wait for the embassy to send our date for the visa interview. The interview was where my first visa application had gone wrong. We hoped it would go better this time with Evan there, but we couldn't count on it. All our experiences so far had led us to expect problems.

One of the additional documents we'd need for the interview was a police clearance report. The report simply verified that I wasn't wanted by the police and attempting to leave the country to escape justice. I felt stupid for not keeping a copy of my report the first time before giving the original to the embassy. The embassy claimed it was impossible to get the original returned or considered for the new application, and the police station didn't keep the report on record. I would have to start the process of obtaining a report over again from the beginning. To do that, we first had to move back to Majnu ka Tilla to be available for residency verification.

I had been avoiding Majnu ka Tilla intentionally. My former roommate was there, a reminder of my guilt over the stolen money.

Despite my reluctance, I'd listed my official residence as a hotel in Majnu ka Tilla, where I knew the owner, and would need to be able to get to the hotel fast when the police came to confirm my residency. We moved at a good time. When we checked to see if the TV was working in our new room, almost every channel was dedicated to coverage of the latest terrorist attack. Multiple bombs had been set off in coordinated attacks at several markets in Delhi. The attacks targeted crowds converging in the narrow lanes of Delhi's markets for the busy shopping season ahead of the Diwali holiday.

Some of the images on the news looked familiar. At a closer look, we recognized Pahar Ganj. A bomb packed in a duffel bag had been left in the luggage rack of a bicycle rickshaw parked at a large intersection. We used to buy fried snacks from a vendor at the corner there. The bomb had gone off at a time we would have been likely to be out in the market, though we didn't necessarily spend much time in the intersection. We were fortunate to have been out of the market that day ourselves, but it felt strange to see news of death and injuries in a place we'd been living. Pahar Ganj was a real place to us. The victims could have been people we'd passed by or had some contact with, like the fried snacks vendor. The vendor was a friendly guy; I hope he is okay.

The same person who'd processed my first police report application also took my case the second time. He recognized me right away and assured us he'd come by the next day to verify my residence. The next day passed, then a week, and he never came. Upon return to the police station, we saw him there, but he pretended not to see us. The secretary asked how much I'd paid him the first time and, when I answered that I'd given him nothing, remarked that it explained why I wasn't having any success now.

As with the marriage office, there came a point when he did have to deal with us. When he finally agreed to see us, he took a brief look at our application before declaring indignantly that we'd submitted insufficient proof of residency. It looked as if he and the judge at the marriage office had attended the same acting school for corrupt bureaucrats. I protested that I'd submitted the exact same information before and he had approved it, without effect.

As a backup plan, we attempted to obtain a clearance document from the Bureau of the Dalai Lama. As the issuing body for my passport, the Tibetan office was technically qualified to issue a clearance document according to the embassy guidelines. All we needed was a piece of paper to show I wasn't a fugitive. We hoped to find a more sympathetic ear at the Tibetan office.

The Tibetan office was no different from Indian offices we'd been to. We had to come back a second time to wait for the person we needed to talk to, and when we did meet with him, he wasn't helpful. I think, in part, he may have been reluctant to interfere in the affairs of the Indian police. The Tibetan government is a guest of India, and I'm sure Tibetan officials have to take that into consideration.

Desperate, I begged and argued with the secretary to find someone able to solve our problem. It was another long wait on another hot day to see the second official that she scheduled us with. Evan's sweat had soaked through his shirt on the long ride to the office to the point that it looked like he'd gone swimming in it. As we waited for the official to see us, I could tell the frustration and pressure was getting to him. Unless this official came up with some sort of document for the embassy, it looked like we might be at a dead end. To an American accustomed to expecting government officials to do their job and having recourse if there's a problem, the roadblock with the police clearance must have been infuriating.

When we were finally allowed into the official's office, he said he'd found our problem; it was that we hadn't submitted sufficient proof of residency to the police station. He scolded us for not following the proper procedure in the first place and continuing to ignore procedure despite the counsel of the other Tibetan official. That was when Evan got up and walked out of the room. After he left, the official told me I should think some more before going to America with Evan since he "looked crazy."

When my unproductive conversation with the official was over, I asked Evan why he'd left the room. He said he'd been mentally weighing the risks and benefits of getting up to punch the official, and as he put it, "I knew it was time to take myself out of the situation."

Evan usually doesn't listen to advice from anyone, but we decided to follow up on an idea from his parents to contact one of his senators. The idea was for the senator's office to communicate with the embassy on our behalf regarding our problem with the police clearance and hopefully impress upon them the seriousness of our application. The senator's office responded quickly, and our contact there was extremely helpful. We were told that the embassy would be willing to consider any documentation from the police station that showed we had at least applied. That sounded realistic and reasonable. Although we'd been skeptical that a senator's office in the U.S. could help with the embassy in Delhi, our contact came through in a big way at a time we felt like the whole world was against us.

Armed with new hope, we returned to the police station. Following an extended runaround at all the local police offices, we came into some luck at the District Commissioner's office. We told the official we didn't expect clearance, we just needed something to show that we'd applied. The official conferred with a few colleagues, then came back with a formal refusal of our application. It wasn't perfect, but we were relieved to have anything at all. We took the formal refusal and hoped for the best at the visa interview.

There was still some time ahead of us. It was November when we received the police report, and the visa interview wasn't until early December. November brought Thanksgiving, a bittersweet holiday for Evan that year. He'd expected to be back to America with me in time for the start of the school year months earlier. Instead, his stay was still dragging on, and with Thanksgiving approaching, he thought more often about home.

We visited frequently with a local friend and her daughters while waiting for the interview. While my friend and I talked, Evan played with the girls. The older daughter, around six at the time, gave Evan some trouble when he was put in charge of watching her. My friend expected her to go off by herself sometimes and was okay with it. Evan thought he couldn't let her out of his sight. I understand now why that was a problem. An American parent would have been furious if Evan couldn't find a child he was responsible for.

I went to the local temple every morning for prayers and tea offerings. Our neighbor, who went out early to sell Tibetan bread, brought Evan back a daily copy of the *Times of India* to read while I was gone. He usually read it on the roof of our building, looking out at the river. It was a beautiful view, though I always felt sorry for the families living in tents on the banks of the river below us.

Early in December, it was finally time for the visa interview. Our feelings were mixed as the interview date approached. This was what we'd been waiting for, yet our uncertainty about the outcome made it a day of as much apprehension as relief. We were about to place our future in the hands of another stranger behind another plastic barrier. Depending on that stranger's judgment, everything we'd been through could either pay off in a lifetime together in America or come to nothing.

It was depressing to think about what would happen if I were to be denied a visa a second time. Our lives had been focused exclusively on this visa for nearly six months, and those months had been a seemingly endless trial of frustrations. We'd been close to giving up more than once before and had kept going. This time, however, if I didn't get the visa, we were not going to start again with a new application.

The night before the interview, Evan and I sat outside on the roof of our building. We were mostly quiet, thinking about what would happen next. When we talked, we talked about what would happen if the embassy said no.

There was a limit to how long Evan could stay with me in India. Our only financial support would have been Evan's dwindling savings and the little money I made as a seamstress. We saw only two options if the embassy said no. One option was to end our relationship; the other was to attempt to cross into Tibet together. The idea of the two of us crossing into Tibet sounds crazy in hindsight, but at the time, it looked like that might be something we'd have to do. Evan and I loved each other, and we'd already been through so much to be together that it didn't seem like we could ever give up and go our separate ways.

On the day of the interview, we arrived at the embassy early to be sure to be near the front of the line when it opened. It would warm up after the sun rose, but in the early morning twilight, the air was still frigid. Though we arrived well before opening, we were not quite the first people there. A small crowd had already gathered outside the embassy gate long before the door opened.

A beggar woman and her two small children came before the crowd. Watching them approaching from a distance, we could see that they were all barefoot as they walked toward us over the freezing asphalt. The children, dressed in ragged and filthy costumes that must have been intended to look festive at one time, had tears running through the makeup on their faces. They put on a performance of sorts, an acrobatic act displaying the flexibility of youth. The miserable children wept and shivered throughout the entire act while making unconvincing attempts at smiles.

The acrobatics of the shivering children in front of this crowd of wealthy professionals was the most heartbreaking display I'd seen. Accustomed to the sight of leprosy, crippled children, blind old men, and skeletal beggars not merely daily, but repeatedly in the course of a single day, it took a particularly shocking confrontation with poverty to affect me. This did it. I gave the mother twenty rupees (equivalent to about fifty cents), a more generous donation than the standard two to five rupees a typical beggar might get at a stoplight. Across from us on the side street, an upscale young Indian couple nudged each other and smirked at us. They no doubt assumed the white man and Asian woman handing out twenty rupees next to the American embassy must be recent arrivals.

The poverty of the shoeless family was something much different and, I think, much worse than our poverty in Tibet. In Tibet, we had land to provide for our needs, and there was always family to support the few people who were unable to take care of themselves. Families shared everything with each other, including with the disabled and elderly. Nobody went hungry or didn't have a bed to sleep in at night.

When the embassy opened that morning, a number of people rushed into line ahead of us as we walked nervously to the entrance. The slow progress of the line to the interview window was excruciating. However long we actually had to wait for our turn, it felt a lot longer.

There were several windows at which the interviews were being held. A single line led up to the windows, feeding the next person to whichever window opened up. We watched the events at the various windows anxiously, looking for signs of the frequency of success and scouting the windows with the most and least friendly workers. Many people in front of us were sent away without visas. There was one window with an old woman who seemed to be rejecting everyone. At the last stretch of the line, we stood next to a seemingly out of place wall-sized photo of a Fourth of July parade in an American small town.

Our interviewer was a young woman, who though not remarkably irritable, was terse and focused on getting through her long day of interviewing as efficiently as possible. She resisted our effort to begin with friendly greetings, cutting right to a demand to Evan to speak louder and speak directly into the small circle of holes through the plastic window. She was initially quite unimpressed with our application.

Although everything was in order, and she never mentioned the police report, she had obvious doubts about the validity of our relationship. The lack of a crowd or an elaborate ceremony in the photos of our wedding was a major concern to her, and her response to our how-we-met story was unenthusiastic. No matter how we explained it, she was sure Evan had bought me drinks at a bar, and then we decided to get married without much in between. I was forced to lie a little by saying my family was not in the wedding photos because they had gone back to Tibet. She was skeptical.

Judging from her questions and expressions during the interview, it looked almost certain she was going to deny my application. The tone of the interview took a sudden and drastic change for the better when she got to the financial cosponsorship documents from Evan's father near the bottom of the pile. Evan's father was working as a lawyer for the state of Maine, and the documents verifying his employment were on state letterhead, prompting our interviewer to ask Evan where he lived there.

She had attended college at the University of Vermont and had made frequent trips up to Portland, Maine, the very city Evan had been living in before coming to India the first time. To explain where he had lived in Portland, Evan mentioned a locally famous bar close to his apartment. Our interviewer had fond memories of that bar. She asked no more questions about the contents of our application, focusing instead on the new conversation about the bar and other favorite locations in Portland. When she and Evan were done talking, she approved my application. We were so happy and relieved we were almost in tears.

She put a green sticker on my passport and sent us to another desk to arrange for the visa to be sent to me when it was ready. I didn't mind paying another four hundred rupees for shipping as long as my passport had a visa in it this time. I gave them the address of a restaurant in Connaught Place partially owned by an older Tibetan I knew. Majnu ka Tilla was not organized with street addresses, making mail very unreliable. I did not want to test my luck with the visa. Like everything in Connaught Place, the restaurant was a fancy establishment. Dorjee, my friend, had bought a share of it and other property in Delhi many years ago when real estate was much cheaper. He was at an age now when he wanted to sell it and retire but had a dilemma: He wanted to sell to a Tibetan, and no Tibetans could afford to come close to offering a fair price.

After a few days, the embassy called to let us know the visa was coming. On the day our visa was scheduled for delivery, we waited outside the restaurant. Fancy restaurants are supposed to be better, but we didn't feel comfortable inside. We were also too cheap to pay for overpriced tea while we waited. My friend Dorjee wasn't there that day anyway.

We missed the courier. Among the customers coming and going, there was one man who went in with a large bag. He didn't appear to be wearing a uniform, or otherwise be easily identifiable as a courier, but when he came back out shortly after going in, I suspected he might be the person we were waiting for. We went inside to ask if anyone had come in with a package and found out someone match-ing the description of the man with the large bag had just left. We ran out to try to catch him, without success.

The courier left a message that he'd be back at ten o'clock the next morning. This time we waited inside the restaurant. Dorjee was there, and we all had tea together. When the package arrived, I was almost afraid to open it. After my last experience receiving a package like this one, I couldn't help but think there could be an unpleasant surprise. This time, the visa was really there. It was hard to believe. After so many days of aggravation, it took a while for the fact that I'd really received the visa to sink in.

My emotions while preparing to leave for America were mixed and complicated. I was excited with the anticipation of a better life with Evan in America and relieved that our struggles at Indian offices were over. At the same time, I was also feeling a certain sadness for what I was leaving behind. My relationship with India had often been unhappy, but there were strong feelings tied to my life there and pieces of that life that were sad to see come to an end. Presented with a choice of a flight out of India leaving the night after we went to buy tickets and one leaving after another week, I would have preferred to stay the extra week to slowly enjoy my last days there. Evan, on the other hand, was more than ready to go. Our regular dealings with corrupt and heartless officials had soured his previously positive view of India. He wanted out, so we chose the earlier flight.

It was harder than I expected to say goodbye to what had been my second home for six years. Refugees like me were not necessarily welcomed in India, but I had to appreciate that India had let me in at all. India had given me my first experience with political freedom and is the country that gave refuge to the Dalai Lama. I was leaving friends behind, people who had known me during difficult times. I was poor in India, but so was everyone else. It was easy to meet people in India and easy to talk. Life was relaxed and social. People were generally friendly and willing to help friends.

The importance of family and close relationships in India reminded me of Tibet. I hadn't worried very much about the future in India because I could depend on any friend to take me in for as long as I needed. I knew of situations in India where people had stayed with a friend for months, or a year, and sometimes years. That support made it easier to take life in stride, no matter how difficult things got. In a country with widespread and severe poverty, I saw little crime or drug use. Problems in India, no matter how serious, were routinely acknowledged with a calm "No problem."

Though I realized I would miss India after all, I was excited to start my new life in America. I wasn't sure quite what to expect, but I was looking forward to it. I packed all the belongings I'd be taking with me into a single suitcase, ready for my fresh start. Going to the airport for our flight felt unreal; I was on the way to get on an airplane that would be in America when I stepped out of it. It seemed unbelievable, almost impossible, considering all the bad luck we'd been having.

We had one last short period of anxiety at the check-in counter. The man at the counter had never seen a Tibetan passport before. He stared at it blankly for a moment, looked at the front, turned it over, flipped through some pages, then told us he'd have to show it to his manager. The manager wasn't sure what to think of it either. It was not the prettiest passport; it looked like something a person could have made on their own. The manager went to find someone who knew what it was. He was gone for what felt like a long time. When he did return, he gave us our boarding passes.

It wasn't until we were through security sitting in the waiting area for our flight to board that we could relax. There were, at last, no more obstacles in front of us. It was finally real and certain: I was headed to America with my husband.

In the waiting area, we overheard an American businesswoman talking loudly into her cellphone. She was incensed that someone had tried to extract a bribe from her in the course of their business dealings. She was proud to have walked out on that person and gone right back to the airport. For most Americans, that was about as much of India's corruption as they could handle.

It was a long flight out of India, but compared to the way I'd arrived, sitting on a plane was easy. It was my first time flying, and I had been looking forward to it. Flying in an airplane sounded exciting. When we were really in the air, I found myself more nauseous than anything else. It was fortunate that the airplane left a bag to vomit into on the back of the seat in front of me. The reality of flying to America was not nearly as much fun as what I'd imagined.

26. A New Life

WE LANDED in Boston on December 9, 2005. Our plane was one of the last to be cleared for landing before the airport canceled all flights due to a heavy snowstorm. Evan's parents were there waiting for us. As we came near the end of the gate, Evan told me he saw his parents. I looked around at all the people waiting, not knowing which ones they were. I didn't know for sure which people were Evan's parents until we were right in front of them.

They welcomed us warmly, eager, I'm sure, both to see their son and to meet this refugee their son had married. Evan's father Dale, a tall, strong man, greeted me with a crushing hug and told me "Welcome home." I was glad to find Dale warmer in person than over the phone. I'd talked to him on the phone once to get a phone number for Evan. He'd quickly given me the number and hung up. It made me think he might be unfriendly. It's possible I called in the middle of the night. I had talked with his mother Diane a few times, and she always seemed nice.

The reflections Evan's parents later related of their first impressions of me emphasized relief. They had been following our efforts to obtain a visa, worrying all the while about how we were faring. Like us, they had come to expect last-minute obstructions to arise. We had been in the very back row of the plane and had taken time

With Dale and Diane in their living room.

going through customs and immigration, giving his parents cause for concern as they watched all the other passengers from the flight come through the gate. When they saw us approaching among the last few stragglers, they were mostly just glad we'd made it.

Diane had a lasting memory of my shoes. Wanting to make the best first impression I could with my old clothes, I'd made sure to wash Delhi's dust off of them in the airport bathroom before meeting Evan's parents. My shoes were still wet while we waited outside for a bus, standing in Boston snow on a freezing day. She told me she'd felt sorry for me, thinking about how cold I must be and how unprepared I was for winter in New England. She'd thought ahead and brought a hat and scarf to the airport for me.

I felt comfortable right away. Being welcomed by Evan's parents did make me feel that I had a home. For six years in India, I had been like an orphan, unable to have a relationship with my parents. Now it felt like I had a family again, though missing my own parents gave me some sadness at the same time.

Evan and I fell asleep on the bus back to his parents' house in

Maine. It had been a long journey to get there, and for the first time in months, we had no pressing worries. Unlike the long flight on the airplane, throughout which I'd been uncomfortable and nauseous, on the bus I could rest. I appreciated that Evan's parents had come down to Boston to meet us at the airport. I imagine it was a long day for them too.

Evan's parents took me out shopping the next day. They bought me warm clothes as well as basics like socks and underwear. In India I hadn't owned many clothes, and I'd left behind some of what I did have. The quality was so poor and the clothes so worn, it didn't seem worth carrying them all the way to America. At one store, Dale offered to hold on to my new bras and underwear while I looked for more. I was surprised—Tibetan family members were embarrassed about those things in front of each other—but I was comfortable with it in the situation because I could see he was being thoughtful.

They also bought me several new pairs of shoes. The quality was much better than anything I'd seen before; the shoes I'd had in Tibet and India usually felt apart soon after I bought them. I did need the clothes, but more than that, it meant a lot to me that they wanted to make sure I had everything I needed. It made me feel like they were showing me love and accepting me into the family.

A few days after I arrived in America, Dale was responsible for co-managing the lunch service at a soup kitchen in Portland. Evan and I went along with his father to help out. The soup kitchen was a totally new and fascinating idea to me. I was impressed with the effort and compassion involved. People came to volunteer there every day, and the work was not easy. Around two hundred people came for lunch the day we were there. It took a lot of cooking to make enough food, and a lot of cleaning when it was over. The quality of the food was surprisingly good. The main course was chicken cordon bleu from a local packaged foods manufacturer, with choices of side dishes, drinks, and cookies for dessert.

Patrons of the soup kitchen were very appreciative, and many of them seemed distinctly embarrassed. At the serving line, people looked down and were shy about asking for the foods they wanted. I wished I could talk with these people to hear their stories. They looked like regular people; I wondered what had happened in their lives to bring them there. If I'd been able to sit down and talk with people, I would have liked to know in particular about their family relationships. A lot of the people were young, with plenty of time to get their lives straight if they had a chance and good advice. It struck me as strange that they didn't have family members to take care of them.

It was right in the middle of the Christmas season. I had never celebrated Christmas before. The best parts of Christmas were the decorated tree with lights and opening presents by the fire. Confused at first about what the tree was doing inside the house, I still was happy to help decorate it and liked the way it looked when it was done. It felt peaceful to watch the blinking lights on the tree at night, especially with a fire in the fireplace. I also liked the surprise of opening presents. There were presents for me, and I didn't have a clue what any of them could be. My favorite presents were a necklace and a stuffed yak toy from Evan's parents. It was nice of them to get me something that reminded me of Tibet.

27. Disappointment with My New Life

WE MOVED OUT to Evan's graduate school in Denver at the end of the holiday season. I went through a difficult time while we were there, feeling isolated and angry with myself for being dependent on Evan for almost everything. In some ways, my experience in America was more difficult than the hardships I'd faced in Tibet and India.

In Tibet and India, I could walk out my door anytime and expect to see people I knew. Socializing was built into everyday life. People traveled on foot, congregated in public spaces, and weren't in a hurry. I would meet friends every time I went out, and we usually ended up having conversations and sharing meals. Because I saw my friends so frequently, we knew each other very well and always felt comfortable around each other.

In Denver, I felt very isolated. The people in our apartment building were nice, the people from Evan's school were nice—everyone was nice—but I wasn't connecting. Planning ahead of time to meet people was strange to me, and when we did spend time with other Americans, it wasn't enjoyable. Few conversations interested me. It took effort for me to follow conversations in English, and I often didn't feel like it was worth it. I'd end up pretending to smile and listen.

While I understood most of what other people said in English, many people found it difficult to understand everything I said to them. I had an accent and often formed English sentences using Tibetan grammar. At times I mixed words from English, Tibetan, and Hindi all in the same sentence. Not being understood was aggravating. I think people probably could have made sense of what I said with a little effort, but the burden of clear communication was on me.

We didn't have a car when we first arrived in Denver and traveled by foot or bicycle frequently. It seemed like we were the only ones. Everyone else was in a car. When everyone is in a car, even a busy city feels empty.

There were a number of Tibetans living in the Denver area, including a friend of mine in a nearby town called Erie. We visited these Tibetan friends at times, which was nice for me, but it wasn't easy to do very often. Traveling without a car was an issue, and so was the fact that most of them, like many Tibetan couples in America, were busy working two low-paying jobs each.

One special exception was when the Dalai Lama came to Denver for a conference of Nobel Prize winners. He held an audience just for Tibetans near Evan's school. Evan and I went with a couple of my Tibetan friends, arriving early to make sure we could get close to the Dalai Lama. The Dalai Lama spoke mostly about the importance of holding on to our culture while living in other countries by doing things like teaching our children our language.

What the Dalai Lama said made sense to me. I knew how difficult it was to hold on to our traditions while living away from home. People would tell me about "taking time to adjust." What they didn't realize was that the cultural barriers I was facing were bigger than adjusting to change. I've never necessarily wanted to be American. I'm a Tibetan, and I want to keep my identity. If adjusting to America meant I had to let go of the identity I already had, I wasn't sure I wanted that.

Along with the isolation I was experiencing, I was also severely self-critical about my lack of independence. America seemed to have a way to do everything with machines that I had no idea how to use. It made me think of an American movie I'd seen in India. In the movie, Arnold Schwarzenegger looked like a person but inside he was really a machine. I started to think maybe Americans were really like that. Seeing all the machines Americans used, and the subdued emotions in their interactions, it looked like the movie could be a true story about America. Sometimes at night I looked over at Evan wondering if maybe he was like that under the skin.

I hated all the machines, making me resistant to learning how to use them. I also hated asking Evan to do things for me and go everywhere with me. It especially bothered me that I was financially dependent. Evan had already spent a lot of money on my visa and coming back to India for me, and I wanted to start doing my part to support us. I didn't like the idea of not being able to function without Evan. If something happened to him, or we separated for some reason, I wanted to be able to take care of myself.

I wanted to find a job right away. If I was going to live in America, I wanted to make money. I needed money to earn back everything Evan had spent on me, and I needed money to help my family back in Tibet. If I couldn't be with them, I thought the best I could do was to help them.

I was disappointed by the experience of looking for a job. Without any verifiable education or work history, finding a job was extremely difficult. For any job in America, the first question the employer always asks is "Do you have experience?" I would apply for simple jobs like cleaning hotel rooms or washing dishes and be asked if I had experience. I didn't mind working hard or learning a complicated job; I just needed a chance. It was ridiculous to me that people were worried about experience for every simple job.

My cultural expectations and difficulty communicating with new people complicated the job hunt. Evan would go with me to hand in applications, and sometimes we'd be able to meet a hiring manager. In Tibetan and Indian society, it's normal for the husband to do the talking when a husband and wife are together. When a manager came over, I'd expect Evan to talk for me. I'd get furious with him for pushing me to talk instead. I felt like he didn't want to take care of me. When I did talk, the busy managers weren't patient about understanding my accent and grammar.

Evan would get frustrated with me for being reluctant to talk. Maybe we'd walked a long way or waited for a bus, and he felt like I hadn't tried to get the job when we got there. We usually ended up arguing when we got back. He was frustrated I'd been quiet, I was angry he hadn't done more to help me out, and we were both frustrated that we weren't having any success.

I was lonely, missing home, and frustrated. I felt stuck. It was painful to me that I couldn't go home. The three years I'd have to wait for American citizenship just to visit my family felt like an impossibly long time.

Evan and I fought at times, making me feel worse about my life and myself. I was only staying in America for Evan, and when we argued, I couldn't see any reason to be here at all. If our relationship wasn't going well, I didn't have any reason to go on with my life. One day during an argument with Evan, I grabbed all the medicine we had and locked myself in the bathroom. Not knowing what most of it was, I swallowed everything. I wanted to die. When I came to America, I'd thought this was my chance to start over with a new and better life. The reality was not working out as I'd planned. I was ready to change to another life; I thought anything would be better. Evan pushed the door open to get inside. He saw the empty medicine bottles in the bathroom and fell to his knees, saying, "What have you done?" I started to feel sorry for him. He was crying, and it showed how much he cared about me.

Evan went to get a cellphone, which I fought to get away from him. He managed to dial 911 before I grabbed it away and threw it across the room. Five or ten minutes later, police were at the door of our apartment to check on the situation. I was amazed they got there so fast and that they'd found us even though Evan hadn't been able to talk to anyone.

The police were very nice. An EMT came, and an ambulance arrived to take me to Denver Health. They gave me IVs right away in the ambulance and brought me to the emergency room. When the nurse brought Evan in, he was relieved to find me in stable condition. In an odd way the suicide attempt brought us closer together. We remembered how much we cared about each other even with all the difficulties we were going through as a couple, and his concern showed me that I could trust Evan to take care of me.

Shortly before I attempted suicide I had found a job, but it was another disappointment, not a solution to my problems. I was working with a daycare that primarily hired immigrants willing to work hard for minimum wage. Many of the other workers were refugees from African countries like Sudan, Somalia, and Ethiopia. My disappointment with the reality of working life had only deepened my disenchantment with America. For working very hard eight hours a day, five days a week, I barely made enough money to keep up with our bills. I'd work all day, come home tired, go back to work the next day, then come home tired again and have nothing to show for it. It was discouraging for me to be working so hard and not be able to save anything. I couldn't picture a future for myself in America spending the rest of my life living like that until I retired.

Between my job at the daycare and Evan's work-study job in maintenance at the university, we were making far more money than I'd ever seen, but most of it quickly disappeared. While it's true we had a more comfortable life with better quality things around us than I'd ever had before, I wasn't enjoying it. Making the equivalent of two dollars a day in India, it had been enough to get by with less money stress than I had in America, and I was able to enjoy my free time more.

When I lived in Tibet, we had to work hard in the summer, then relaxed through the winter. We never had to worry about being able to pay bills. Most of the time we didn't deal with cash at all. We could do everything ourselves; we didn't have to depend on anyone else for a job or to get what we needed.

Doing hard work in Tibet as a family had been much more enjoyable for me than working for a boss at a job and being tired by the time I came home to spend time with my family. In America, work was focused on work. I found myself spending most of my time in an environment without meaningful relationships, and I didn't have much time and energy left over for the relationships I did care about.

The daycare where I worked wasn't hiring immigrants as a charity. The management knew they could push immigrants to work hard for every hour of the workday and pay them very little for it. They cared more about saving money than anything else. One of the other ways they saved money was by giving the kids cheap food. Most of the food was whatever had gone past the sell-by date at the local supermarket. They had some deal going with the supermarket to get the food at a discount. Most of it was canned food. Sometimes the young kids were given spaghetti for lunch even though they couldn't get much of it in their mouths. After half an hour, lunch would be over and the food taken away. If they were still hungry, too bad. Breakfast usually wasn't substantial and didn't keep the kids full for long. The young kids usually started howling before lunchtime, and the older ones stared in the window from the playground, waiting to be called in for lunch.

When kids were naughty, they were grabbed by the back of their shirt and pulled to the corner. If they wouldn't walk, they were dragged. My supervisor did that more than anyone. Then, when the parents came to pick up the kids, she acted very sweet and nice with the kids and parents. The second the parents left, her face totally changed. When I first started, I thought she looked like a nice person. Once I realized what kind of person she was underneath her fake smile, I didn't like her at all.

Some kids arrived as soon as we opened, around six o'clock, and were still there almost until we closed at eight. The ones who arrived at six usually got tired long before naptime. We had to keep waking them up until it was time to let them sleep. At lunch, they would eat a few bites then fall asleep at the table. All this time the kids spent at daycare made them look to the staff for love.

On one occasion, a child ignored his mother's arrival at the same time I was getting ready to leave. He showed no interest in going to his mother and then, when he saw me leaving, wanted to come with me. He was a sweet, chubby kid. He held his arms out to me to come pick him up. I told him it was time to go see Mommy and I'd see him tomorrow. He still wanted to leave with me. I gave him a hug and told him he needed to go see Mommy now. My supervisor later told me I should have simply left quietly.

A good thing that came out of that experience was that it made me more interested in having my own children. Until then, I thought I definitely did not want to have kids ever. Seeing how sweet and affectionate kids could be changed my mind. I starting looking forward to the day I had my own kids to love. It was also nice to work with the refugees from Africa. Despite the distance between our homelands, the African immigrants and I had a lot in common. Most of them were from small villages like mine and were struggling to accept their new life in America.

I also worked a much better part–time job helping an older woman, Laura, with various tasks like laundry and organization. She was a very kind woman, and I always enjoyed our time together. She was patient and did a good job showing me what she needed me to do. If she didn't understand something I said, she asked me to try again without rushing me. She was interested in my history and cared about me beyond just being my boss. It's been years since I've left Denver now, and we still keep in touch.

There was one time when she gave me a small job to do and told me to wait for a little bit while she went out to see a friend. I finished the job quickly and then wasn't sure what to do. I sat down on the couch to wait for her and fell asleep. Three hours passed before she came back, and I slept through all of it. She was very apologetic about being gone so long and didn't say anything about finding me asleep. She happily paid me for the entire time, including the nap.

28. Tenzin Yangchen

INSPIRED IN PART by my job at the daycare, I took an increasing interest in becoming a mother. I needed something positive to focus on to sustain me in America. I was thinking about my family back in Tibet every day, but I couldn't be with them. If I was seriously going to spend the rest of my life in America, I needed a new family to love as much as the one I'd left behind in Tibet. Evan had major reservations about the idea. He hadn't spent much time around children in his life, and he wasn't certain he was cut out to be a father. He was also worried about having a baby at a time when our life was unstable and we weren't financially secure. He wanted to wait and think about it again later.

I found Evan's logic typically American, and aggravating. I knew everything would be fine as long as we loved each other and any baby we had together. I couldn't see why Americans like to follow a recipe for everything in life. Sometimes the best plan is to go ahead and do something and live with it.

We told Evan's parents on the phone that we were talking about having a baby. They said very clearly that they didn't think it was a good idea. They had the same concerns as Evan. I suspect they were also concerned by my suicide attempt. The concerns of Evan and his parents did not change my mind. Although I do believe in listening to advice from parents, that doesn't mean I always agree with the

advice after listening to it. I can be strong-minded if I am comfortable with something I'm thinking about, even if other people close to
me think it's a bad idea. That was true when I became a nun, when
I went to India, and when I pursued my relationship with Evan, and
it was true when I wanted a baby.

Evan ultimately agreed. When we found out I was pregnant, it
was exciting, and it made us nervous. We recognized that this was
going to change our lives completely from that point on. The idea of
being responsible for a new life was more than a little intimidating.

Evan was getting close to completing the coursework portion of
his graduate studies during the early part of my pregnancy. He would
only have his master's thesis left to work on by the baby's due date.
When the baby came we wanted to be near his family, so he made
arrangements with the school to complete his thesis off site. In the
end, he never finished the thesis. With the complication in our life
and a new baby, he couldn't give it the focus it needed, and it wasn't
realistic for him to apply for doctoral programs in our circumstances.

On a snowy day at the end of November, we packed our belongings into our car, which we'd brought from Maine to Denver not long
before, and headed to the East Coast. I was seven months pregnant
when we left. Traveling most of the way across the country while
that far along in my pregnancy wasn't comfortable. For most of the
drive I was hungry, I had to pee, and my back hurt.

We stopped on the way to visit a friend of mine in Madison, Wis-
consin, staying for several days. While we were there, my friend's
husband told me a disgusting but funny story about childbirth that
I unfortunately remembered when giving birth to my own daughter.
Someone he knew had a problem during childbirth in India. She
was in a small room, with the foot of the delivery bed very close to
the wall. The woman had to poop at the same time the baby was
coming. She tried to hold it, but couldn't. She was pushing the baby
and holding the poop until she gave up and pushed both. When the

woman stopped holding the poop in and pushed it too, it came fly-ing out and got stuck on the wall. The embarrassed husband tried to wipe it up, smearing it instead. When he was done wiping, it looked like someone had used poop to paint the wall.

After leaving Madison, we drove nonstop to Maine. We stayed with Evan's parents until he could find work and an apartment. The job he found had him working in a school with children with developmental disabilities, primarily autism. It was a job he took in part to work in an area where he believed he could provide valuable service, but mostly because it was a job that was hiring. With a baby on the way, we needed an income.

I went into labor shortly before Evan's job started. When my water broke, my first thought was that I must have peed in the bed. I woke up to a wet bed and wasn't sure what happened. I was embarrassed and didn't want to tell Evan about it. I put down a towel and tried to go back to sleep. The contractions started a little later. Being late at night, I still didn't wake Evan up right away. As the contractions became more frequent and intense, I began to suspect I was get-ting close to delivery and woke up Evan. He was surprised and a little worried—it was three weeks before the due date. He called the on-call number for the doctor and was advised to take me straight to the hospital.

Daylight was breaking as we arrived at the hospital. Though the delivery room was quite nice, I wasn't in a position to enjoy it. The contractions continued getting closer and stronger through the morning. The pain was intense, so much so I was having second thoughts about having the baby. It didn't seem fair that I had to be in so much pain while Evan was totally fine. Evan's boss in Denver had warned him to expect me to put him in a headlock and punch him in the face repeatedly while yelling, "You did this to me!" as the baby came out. I didn't exactly do that, but I understood the impulse!

I was thinking about the story my friend's husband told me about the unfortunate situation in the Indian delivery room. It felt like I needed to poop when the baby was coming out, and I did not want events in the story to happen to me. The doctor was right down close to me, making me more concerned about putting anything unpleasant in her face. I wanted to go to the bathroom, then come back and push the baby, but the doctor wouldn't allow it. Ultimately, with the baby coming out, there was nothing else to do but push. To my relief, there was no poop involved.

I was so happy to see the baby when she came out. My cousin in Norbulingka had helped us get a name for her through the Dalai Lama's offices. The Tibetan custom is to ask lamas to name our babies. Part of Tibetan names comes from the lama's own name, and part is given by the lama. We believe that lamas know the perfect name to fit each child. Tibetans say that parents who name their own babies tend to have unhealthy and cranky children. When parents of these unhealthy and cranky children go to a lama to change the child's name, they see significant improvement.

I don't know what his role was exactly, given that the Dalai Lama can't possibly have time to carefully consider every name requested from him, but the Dalai Lama was involved in choosing our daughter's name: Tenzin Yangchen. Tenzin comes from the Dalai Lama's religious name, Tenzin Gyatso, and Yangchen is a female bodhisattva associated with music and the arts. We call her by the affectionate name Tenny. One of our initial reactions when we received her name was that we thought she was never going to be a musician, as the name Yangchen suggested. Evan and I are the worst singers either of us has ever met. Her talent for drawing, however, is incredible. Yangchen truly is the right name for her.

All the pain of childbirth was quickly forgotten when I saw Tenny. It was amazing to look at her baby feet and baby hands. Everything about her was so tiny. Holding my daughter for the first time was a strange and wonderful feeling. I couldn't believe I'd really made a baby. I was pretty proud of myself.

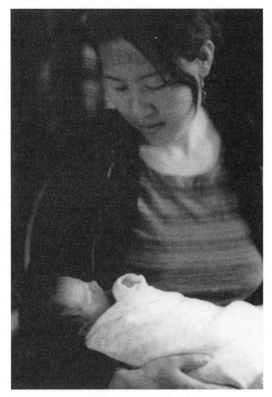

Me holding Tenzin Yangchen.

The nurses showed me how to breastfeed. It made me nervous because Tenny was tiny and I had to be so gentle. Her tiny mouth was having trouble sucking out my milk. To make sure she was getting enough food right away, the nurses used tubes to feed her through her nose. She hated the tubes. Her tiny hands kept trying to grab the tubes and pull them out. With practice, she did get the hang of breastfeeding, and once she got it, she was hooked. She wanted to breastfeed all the time. For the first couple of weeks it seemed like anytime she woke up, breastfeeding was all she could think about. It worked well. She ate and ate and got bigger and bigger.

Leaving the hospital with our new baby was unbelievable. Here was a tiny little new person, and they were letting us just take her home with us. She was so small we had to use three rolled-up blankets to make her snug in the car seat. That first time actually taking our baby out on our own brought a heavy sense of new responsibility. I felt like somebody should be coming along to check on us to make sure we were doing a good job taking care of her.

I was very happy to have my daughter and very overwhelmed thinking about being responsible for her. I wished that new mothers in America were taken care of for a month like new mothers in Tibet. In Tibet the entire family gives a new mother special care for one month after delivering a baby. We believe the new mother has done something very special bringing a new life into the world and deserves a rest. One week after Tenny was born, Evan had to start his new job, leaving me to fend for myself and care for the new baby alone for most of the day. Tenny had to breastfeed every couple of hours all day and night and needed diaper changes about as often. I was tired from the pregnancy to start with, was not getting enough sleep, and all the breastfeeding was making me sore.

We soon moved to our new apartment in Brunswick, Maine. It was a small apartment by American standards, just one bedroom with a small living room and tiny kitchen, but it was no less room than I was used to having in Tibet and India. The difference for me was the feeling of isolation. I was home all day with Tenny, still did not have a driver's license, and didn't have many friends or family around for support. Sometimes the apartment felt like a jail, especially in winter. In the summer, I could take the stroller and go for a walk around the neighborhood or downtown. That wasn't practical in the winter. I was in a free country, but I felt trapped. With time on my hands, I thought about Tibet and my family there. I wished I could go back and be with them.

Most nice days, we went out for a walk when Evan came home from work. Our neighborhood was peaceful and pretty, and very quiet. It was the kind of neighborhood where people we saw outside typically smiled and said hello when we walked by, but I could never get used to how few people we saw. I got the feeling that everyone was doing something together and we hadn't gotten the message. That happened sometimes in Tibet. Once in a while, the entire village was supposed to be working on a project, and a few people didn't hear about it. When they went out and didn't see any activity, they would know right away something was wrong. That's how I felt anytime we walked around our neighborhood.

I got the idea we needed to make a friend for Tenny. Although our situation still wasn't all that stable, we loved having Tenny and were sure we'd love another baby. It looked like, in America, it's important to have a brother or sister for kids to have someone around to play with. From a very young age, Tenny loved other kids. Any time we saw other kids at the park or playground, she was very focused on the other kids she saw, making me feel sorry for her when we came home and she only had Evan and me to play with. We were more confident now because of our positive experience with Tenny, and we decided to have another baby.

29. Tenzin Yangzom

WHILE I WAS pregnant with our second child, I was also studying for the American citizenship test. I couldn't wait to become a citizen so I could go home to see my family. Traveling into Chinese-occupied Tibet with my Tibetan passport wasn't an option. In order to receive an American passport, I had to wait for three years from the date of my marriage, then apply to be a U.S. citizen and pass the test.

Evan's mother helped me study the list of one hundred possible test questions. The information was all new to me and used a lot of specialized vocabulary. It was discouraging that most Americans who looked at any of the questions usually said, "Oh, you don't really need to know that." Being pregnant, I was tired and did not enjoy learning all this new information, but it was important to me to make sure I passed the test on my first try. I was lucky to have Diane to push me to keep studying. Many days I didn't feel up to it. I would have liked to study tomorrow, and as they say in India, tomorrow never comes.

Close to the due date for our second child we went back to stay with Evan's parents temporarily. I still didn't drive, and we wanted to be sure I would have a way to get to the hospital if I had a problem or the baby started coming while Evan was at work. It was also more convenient for Diane to take me to prenatal checkups, which were becoming frequent as the due date approached.

On weekends, Dale always had a good breakfast, like waffles and bacon with tea (and coffee for everyone else), ready when I got up. Raised on a dairy farm, Dale was an early riser. He'd have everything set and ready to eat before I came downstairs. That's nice anytime. While pregnant, I usually woke up starving. Having a big breakfast waiting for me in the morning while I was pregnant was fantastic.

The day my second daughter was born, I experienced pains in the morning with some blood in my urine. Diane called the doctor's office and made an appointment for two o'clock that afternoon. At the appointment I wasn't seen by my regular doctor. The new doctor told us that everything was fine and the baby wouldn't be coming for another week or two. I happened to have an ultrasound appointment that same day at four o'clock. When we arrived at the ultrasound appointment, I was told that I was having contractions and should go to the hospital right away. I'm glad I had that ultrasound appointment, or I'm not sure what would have happened. The ultrasound technicians were right: My baby was on the way.

On the way to the hospital, I told Diane about a report I saw on the news about a woman who went to a hospital after having contractions, only to be turned away and told the baby wasn't coming yet. The hospital was wrong, and her baby was born on her way home. Diane said we were lucky we didn't end up on the news too.

At 10:40 that night, my second daughter was born. She was also named by the Dalai Lama. Her name is Tenzin Yangzom. We call her Zoom. When she was almost ready to come out, I screamed very loud. I couldn't hold it in. A male doctor from the hospital turned to me and said, "Shh." I couldn't believe it. He had no idea how hard it is to push out a baby. It's a lot easier to say "shh" than push the baby out, and if I wanted to scream, I was going to do it. I turned to Evan very seriously to tell him that no matter what I said later, this was our last baby; I wasn't doing this again. The only way we were having another baby was if doctors find a way for a man to be pregnant.

Tenny, who was two at the time, was very affectionate with Zoom from the beginning. When Tenny came to visit the hospital the next day, she gave Zoom kisses and lots of attention. Later, after returning home, Tenny tried to help Zoom by showing her where to find her eyes, ears, and nose. Anytime she went to sleep, Tenny needed to be next to Zoom. If she woke up and Zoom wasn't there, she'd get very upset and yell, "Baby! Baby!"

A few months before Zoom was born, we started putting Tenny in her own bed. Until that point, she had always slept with Evan and me, an arrangement we were happy with and was convenient while I was breastfeeding her. Evan's parents, supported by some parental-advice resources and our doctor, had been encouraging us for a long time to put Tenny in her own bed. It was supposed to make her more independent, and we were told it was going to be harder to put her in her own bed the longer we waited. With a second child coming, we gave in and decided to make Tenny sleep in her own bed before Zoom came to join us.

It was the worst decision we've made as parents. Tenny hated going to her own bed, and she was too young to understand why we were kicking her out. The only way she would sleep in her own bed was if someone stayed there with her until she was asleep. That job usually fell on me, since Evan couldn't manage to sneak out of the room without waking her up again. It did take some focus to sneak away. Tenny held on to our clothes and would sit up suddenly if she started falling asleep to make sure we didn't try to leave.

Our doctor told us that we needed to let her cry for fifteen minutes, then very quickly get her to settle down and leave again. We tried that. It was a horrible feeling to lie in bed listening to Tenny cry without going to comfort her. She would howl as loud as she could. Her crying would go on for fifteen minutes, stop when we came to her room, and then start right back up again as soon as we left her alone. It broke our hearts to listen to that.

Being pregnant, I was tired and ready for sleep at night myself.

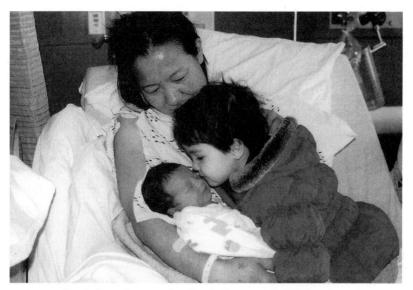

Tenzin Yangchen meeting Tenzin Yangzom for the first time.

I wasn't thrilled about staying awake to help Tenny, and I was no more excited about getting up during the night to start the process again if she awoke to find no one there. None of us were getting much sleep, and the situation was creating tension. I was frustrated with Tenny for keeping us up at night, and frustrated with Evan for not doing a better job helping Tenny fall asleep without waking her again. I would tell Evan how to do it, and he didn't want to listen. Evan didn't agree with putting Tenny in her own bed in the first place, so he was frustrated with me for pushing this on her. Tenny was frustrated about us kicking her out of our bed and leaving her alone. She also became crankier during the day from the decrease in sleep she was getting.

I wasn't really comfortable insisting on putting Tenny in her own bed if she weren't ready, but I didn't trust my own judgment. Even though I didn't understand it, I thought we needed to follow the advice of elders. If one person with experience had told me I didn't have to put her in her own bed, I wouldn't have wanted to do it.

Nobody was getting enough sleep, and nobody was happy. In the end, I finally found one person who told me we didn't have to be doing this. During a prenatal doctor's visit, I explained our problem to a nurse, who said it was okay to let her back in our bed if no one was getting sleep.

Once that nurse said it was okay, we let Tenny back in to our bed that same night. She was still there after Zoom's birth. To accommodate the crowd, we turned our bed sideways to make room for everyone. It made our feet cold at night, but we were happier with cold feet than listening to Tenny cry. We all loved each other and liked being close. We never told Evan's parents about Tenny coming back in the bed. I suspect at some point they may have noticed our bed was turned sideways and figured it out, but they never said anything. Contrary to what we'd been told, Tenny eventually moved out of our bed without an issue. When she was almost four years old, Tenny voluntarily went to her own bed. She was ready, and she was old enough to discuss what was happening.

In Tibet and India, I had never heard of the terrible twos. A lot of people in Tibet and India have many kids (though this is now limited by government controls in Tibet), but they don't have an issue with terrible twos. We'd never had a problem with Tenny either until we put her in her own bed. Then she started having trouble, and we thought, "Oh, this must be the terrible twos." After we let her back in our bed, she was a perfect child again. It makes me think that young children in America have a hard time because parents push too much independence on them early.

In Tibet it would be strange for kids not to sleep in the same bed as their parents. I think it may be one of the cultural differences between Tibet and America. In America, personal independence is considered important. In Tibet, family relationships are important. Families are supposed to stay together in Tibet; parents don't expect their kids to grow up to live completely separate lives.

30. My Struggle to Return to Tibet

I TOOK THE citizenship test while Zoom was still very small, before she could crawl. The people working at the Homeland Security office where I took the test were very unfriendly people. It looked like they got paid more to be cranky, like maybe it was part of a strategy to discourage immigration. On the day of my appointment, I was sent in to see a man in an office. I walked in and said hi to the man administering the test. Without any greeting at all, the man looked up from some papers and started asking me questions. It took me by surprise at first; I wasn't sure I'd heard him right. I was used to Americans starting with some brief small talk to set a comfortable tone, and this person hadn't so much as returned my hello. He might have been having a busy day, but it doesn't take long to say hi back to someone.

To pass the test I had to correctly answer six out of ten questions and write a simple sentence in English. The man in the office asked me six questions and had me write the sentence "Columbus Day is in October," then he said, "We're done here." I had to ask if I'd passed or not. I was very excited when he said yes, and I told him so and thanked him. There was no "You're welcome" or anything like that, just, "Be here tomorrow at nine o'clock." I asked if I could take care of whatever it was I needed to do that same day (Zoom had a doctor's appointment the next morning), but he said no. It wasn't easy to get more than a few words out of this person. Before I left, he gave me some papers that explained what would happen in the morning. It was the citizenship oath ceremony.

Back at home, Evan and I broke out a special bottle of champagne we'd saved for the occasion. The long, aggravating, and expensive process of immigration to America was complete at last, and my dream of going back to Tibet to see my family was coming closer. I had been away from home for twelve years.

Shortly after I first arrived in India, I had sent a letter to my parents letting them know I had arrived safely and was attending school. That first letter successfully made it to my family in Tibet. Several other letters that mentioned the exile government and the Dalai Lama never arrived. My parents sent only one letter to me. It was short but heartfelt. It was probably the only letter they've ever sent. Like every letter that entered India from China, the envelope had been obviously opened and taped back together.

For years, those two letters were the only communication I had with my family. I had no way to know how my family was doing, and my parents had no way to know if I were dead or alive. Other people in my village thought I was dead. Though no one ever said that directly in front of my family, they knew what people thought.

About five years after I left Tibet, one of my cousins crossed into India. He came while I was living on my own in McLeod Ganj, a little while before I met Evan. My adopted brother Yula had acquired a telephone since I left, and my cousin had the number. He gave me the number, providing my first chance to talk with my family since the day I left my village.

After Yula picked up and I told him who was calling, he immediately asked where I was. He seemed to think I was on the way home, maybe calling from Lhasa. When I told him I was still in India, he was angry with me. He said, "What the hell are you doing? Don't you want to come home and see your parents before they die?" In Tibet, it is extremely important to be with your parents when they are old; you absolutely need to go see them when they are sick and getting close to death. Yula did have a point, but what could I do?

I had to keep the conversation brief because it was very expensive for me to call Tibet. Before we hung up, I mentioned that I was eager to talk to my mother. Unfortunately Yula followed that request quite literally and brought my mother back to the city with him without telling my father I'd called. My mother and father lived in different houses with two of my brothers in the same village, so my father didn't know anything until later. When he found out I'd called, he complained to Yula for not telling him, and was told I had only asked to talk to my mother. That hurt my father a lot.

My mother's first words to me were, "I knew you were alive." I felt sorry for the sadness and difficulty she'd experienced because I left home. We talked for half an hour, as long as I could afford. That was the only time we spoke until I arrived in America; it was too expensive for me to call again. Not long after I came to America, my parents' village was connected to telephone wires. My parents couldn't decide which house to put the phone in, so they each got one. That was better; I could hear their voices, but that wasn't the same as seeing them in person.

I applied for a visa to enter China right after receiving American citizenship and an American passport. We applied for visas for the whole family through a visa agency because the Chinese consulate does not accept applications by mail. Soon after submitting the materials, we received a phone call saying that Evan was approved for a visa, and that they needed us to fax copies of the birth certificates for our daughters. The woman from the agency told us everything was fine, they only needed to show a little additional documentation. A short time later, we received another phone call; there were problems with my visa application. The woman from the agency was perplexed. She talked with Evan at length, looking for clues to the origin of the problems. We were applying for a standard tourist visa, which should have been easy to get. Finally, one question solved the mystery: The woman on the phone asked Evan if I were Tibetan. She guessed that the consulate was creating a delay to give them time to check whether I was, in her words, "a good Tibetan or one of the bad Tibetans." They must have concluded I was a bad Tibetan, as I did not receive a visa.

We tried applying through a different agency with the same result. The bad news took everything out of me. I couldn't get out of bed; I couldn't even lift my hand up from the bed. I was just about broken. Seeing my parents again had been the focus of my life, and I had come so close. I couldn't believe they wouldn't let me go back just for a short time to see my family. I wasn't involved with any political groups, I wasn't going to protests, and I didn't want to go to Tibet to make any trouble. I only wanted to see my family. I had waited all these years, and I couldn't see how another human being could deny me the chance to see my aging parents.

I was feeling very unhappy about my situation at that point. I couldn't have the one thing I wanted most, to see my family, and I wasn't fitting in well in America. I didn't have a sense that America was the right place for me to be, but I couldn't see any other options.

It gave me some consolation that Evan and his family had been very good to me. Evan is a good husband and a good father. A lot of women are looking for someone like that, and only the lucky ones ever find someone. I appreciated everything that Evan and his family had gone through for me. His parents had treated me like their own daughter from the beginning.

The problem was that no amount of kindness from them could make my feelings for my family back home disappear. Differences between me and my American family made it hard for me to be as close with them as I was with my family in Tibet, even though I've been treated much better in America. I've been through experiences with my family in Tibet that most Americans aren't able to relate to no matter how hard they try to understand. I've also grown up with very different habits. These differences in cultural habits can leave me feeling lonely in America. Sometimes I feel like no one else cares about the things that are important to me, and I'm not interested in the things that are important to them.

One of the big differences, which is also my biggest complaint with American culture, is that Americans often avoid talking about emotions. I get the impression that Americans think everybody's feelings are their own business. I believe that part of caring about a person is wanting to listen to how that person is feeling and know what that person is thinking about. Unless you know people's deep feelings and what's on their minds, it's hard to really know each other and have close relationships.

I found that Americans were surprised and often uncomfortable if I mentioned negative emotions I was feeling. That was never a problem in Tibet. In Tibet we usually told each other what we were feeling, especially when upset or angry. Although a lot of the time that led to heated arguments or being told to stop being stupid and feel differently about something, it was all real. The arguments and the criticisms made our relationships stronger because we knew what friends and family really thought. In America, it seemed like people tried to make everyone around them happy, but in a way that hid their true feelings. I didn't see how Americans could really understand each other if they kept their feelings hidden.

It was the same with talking about serious issues. Talking about the situation in Tibet or any other serious issue made many people uncomfortable as well. What usually happened when I talked about Tibet was that people looked very concerned for a moment and said, "That's too bad." In the next breath, they would change the conversation to something stupid like a TV show. Some people seemed to think there are more important issues at stake on reality TV shows than there are in Tibet.

The area where my difficulty talking about deep feelings has caused me the most frustration has been with addressing problems in my marriage. It's possible to love someone very much and be driven completely crazy by that same person. My marriage with Evan has always had special difficulties. We're from different cultures, we've had different life experiences, and we have different habits. It can be hard to understand each other, and we don't know many people who can relate to our issues.

There have been a number of times Evan and I have been so fed up with each other that we thought seriously about divorce. We love each other, but sometimes it's hard for us to live together. Part of the problem is that, when there is any difficulty or unhappiness in life, it's easiest to blame whoever is closest to the situation. When I'm going through a hard time, I get angry with Evan, who gets angry with me for being angry with him. I think I'm totally right and he's totally wrong, and Evan thinks the opposite.

If we were in Tibet, I could walk out and stay with my parents until Evan was ready to come get me and work out our issues. When he came to get me, it wouldn't be only our problem. We would both have to explain what we were arguing about to my parents and any older siblings present, describing exactly what happened, how we were feeling, and what we were thinking. Older people would tell us what we were doing wrong and what we needed to do to improve the situation.

In Tibet, one family member's problems are important to the whole family, and they sincerely try their best to help a couple work through any difficulties they're having. If their child is part of the problem, Tibetan parents will say so. When my sister threw a bowl of thukpa at her husband during an argument, for example, my parents told her she couldn't expect the situation to improve if she does that. I don't know how well Evan would take advice from older people (I affectionately call him the Tibetan word for goat head, ramagu, because he is so stubborn), but I would be very happy to have someone tell me when I was doing something wrong and let me know what I needed to change.

I wish my parents-in-law took some of the responsibility for resolving problems in our marriage. It's hard to talk with them about our relationship problems, and they don't have much to say if something comes up. When I fight with Evan, and there's no one to help us fix it, I don't know where to go. If I don't have somewhere to go, it's hard to get away from the problem long enough to calm down and think about making things better.

Although separation from my family in Tibet was always on my mind and exacerbating my difficulties with life in America, I let a long time go by before I considered applying a third time for a visa. The disappointment of another rejection would be too much for me to handle. I thought the only thing to do was to try my best to focus on the family I had with me. I did try my best, and I do love my American family very much, but it wasn't easy for me to let go of my longing to return to Tibet.

Knowing that my family in Tibet was living very simply, I couldn't enjoy comforts in America. Our habit at home had always been to share everything in common, and I didn't see why I should have anything now that my family could not have too. I didn't want to put myself above my family by living at a different level. I thought if I couldn't be with my family, the best I could do was to give them some of what I had, so Evan and I sent my family whatever we could afford, especially things like comfortable shoes and warm jackets. Evan's parents also helped by giving us items to send and donating money for my father to distribute in the village. For a long time, it looked like maybe that would be the closest relationship I could have with my family.

When the Dalai Lama came to New York City for a teaching, it gave me a reason to go to New York anyway, and while I was there, I would be close to the Chinese consulate. With some reluctance, I decided to try applying for a visa in person at the consulate in New York. Under those circumstances, at least I wouldn't feel like I had come to New York for nothing if I were to be denied again, and the Dalai Lama teaching would give me something positive to think about.

Evan was working, so our two girls came with me. When I first saw New York, I thought it must be impossible for Tibetans from small villages like mine to live in such a crowded place. The area where I went to stay with Tibetan friends was different from my first impression of the city. Populated entirely by Asians, less organized, and with more trash around, it made me feel like I was in Delhi again.

I spent a night at an apartment of some friends. One of the men living there had been stuck for years, waiting for a resolution to his application for refugee status. Until then, he couldn't get American citizenship and he couldn't go back to Tibet. Homeland Security was holding on to his passport until his status was resolved and had been doing so for five years. His wife and kids were still in Tibet all this time. Zoom was bothered by bedbugs during our night there, causing her to howl almost all night. I was embarrassed and apologized to everyone. The man replied, "Are you kidding me? I was so happy to hear the sound of children."

At the Dalai Lama teaching, it felt like I was spending a moment home in Tibet because there were so many Tibetan people there wearing chubas. Tenny was three and a half, maybe old enough to remember the experience. She knew I was excited to see the Dalai Lama (or as she called him, the "Dawa Dama"), so she was too. Whether either of the girls remembers it or not, I'm glad they had the experience of seeing the Dalai Lama and hope they are able to see him again in the future.

At the consulate, I went to a special office that specifically handles visa applications by Tibetans. The person working there took down all my information, including information about my family. The information was sent to China for the local police to investigate my history and my family before the consulate could make a decision. When the investigation was complete, I heard back from the consulate: This time they had approved my visa. With my visa approved, visas for Evan and the kids were quick and easy.

31. Reunited with My Family

WE BOUGHT our tickets right away for a date a month later when Evan would be able to get time off from work. With our tickets ready and a specific date approaching when we would really go to Tibet, the one-month wait for Evan's time off wasn't easy. The chance to see my family again had become real and in reach. Counting the days until our flight seemed to pass a lot slower than regular time.

I was a little nervous about traveling with our girls. Young children need a lot of care and can easily get sick. Our girls weren't used to living in Tibet, and I would have felt terrible if they had any health issues while we were there.

They behaved surprisingly well on the airplane, considering that they spent a total of almost forty hours in travel. An airplane is a tough place for kids since they can't get up and run around to work out their energy. The hardest part was our arrival in Beijing. We had to drag the kids through customs and all over the airport, then catch a bus to another airport to catch our plane to Xining, the closest to my family we could get by plane. We had six hours between our arrival in Beijing and our flight out, and we needed most of it. We were lucky a friend of mine met us at the airport, or we would have had a lot of trouble figuring it all out on our own.

Beijing was screaming hot and crowded, and the water faucets in the airport bathroom didn't work. In a way, that all made me feel good. It reminded me I was really in China. I wasn't home yet, but I knew I was on my way.

Our arrival at the final airport in Xining was when I first had the feeling that I'd made it home. It was a good thing we didn't have any more flights after that one, because Tenny was finally fed up. When we woke her up to get off the plane, she didn't want to go. She told us she didn't want to go anywhere; she was tired. In spite of a lack of sleep, I felt the opposite. I was incredibly energized.

The airport in Xining was small. Waiting for our bags to come out on the only baggage carousel, I saw Yula waiting for me behind the gate. He waved to me, and tears came to both our eyes. Then it was real. I was seeing one of my family members for the first time in twelve years. There's no way to describe how that felt.

From the airport, we were still about a six- or seven-hour drive away from Yula's home in Guinan. He brought a friend with a car to the airport to drive us to his house. It turned out the friend did not know his way around the city. It also appeared that he did not have much experience with city driving. He would get us completely lost, get back on track, and then get lost again. Each time he realized he'd made a mistake, he made U-turns wherever he was in the road; it didn't matter if he were on a highway or crossing an intersection. I was just thinking, "Come on, hurry up and get me home."

Around 3:30 in the morning we arrived at Yula's house. Yula had called ahead to let his family know when we would arrive, and they were all outside waiting for us when we got there. Yula's two sons had come home from school for my visit, and his older son's wife and baby were living there. My brother Dukher and my sister had also come to Guinan to meet me, also waiting outside the house at 3:30 in the morning to see us come in. Dukher said he'd spent all night watching the clock and waiting for us.

Everyone was crying when we arrived. We don't give hugs in Tibet, but I could see everyone's feeling. We looked at each other's faces with our eyes full of tears. After twelve years apart, it felt like they had come back from the dead, and they felt the same about me. That moment of seeing my family members waiting outside Yula's house was one of the most special experiences of my life.

A large spread of food was ready for us inside the house. There were fruits and breads, freshly cooked momos, and a plate of meat. After eating, we talked for a long time until my family insisted we must be tired and needed to go to bed. We were shown our bed, but we couldn't sleep. Yula, Dukher, and my sister all came to the bed-room with us, and we continued talking for a long time. Although I'd assumed Evan already had a good idea about Tibetan habits from everything I'd told him, he was surprised when my brothers and sister stayed on the bed with us. He had been expecting to actually get some sleep.

There was a place nearby where we could pay to use the show-ers; Evan and I went there in the morning to wash up. The showers weren't great, and after a few days in Tibet, we felt fine without showers at all. Despite never showering, Tibetans are not at all stinky. My mother–in–law once guessed that Tibetans don't find each other stinky because everyone smells the same way. If that were true though, we would have noticed an odor when we first arrived. I don't know how it happens, but I'm reasonably sure Tibetans smell fine despite working outside all day and never showering afterward. My best guess is that the open environment and dry climate have something to do with it.

When we came back from our showers, we learned that Chinese secret policemen had come to the house looking for me. The local police had known I was coming to the area because they'd had to clear me for my visa application, but they did not know the exact day I was arriving. Even if they had known, they had no way to know where I was planning to stay the first night. I think the only way the

My mother at Kobi's house with Kobi mixing butter and barley flour
behind her, my sister on the bed, and Zondija's daughter.

secret police could have known when and where to look for me was
by listening to Yula's phone. My calls to Tibet from America were
always disconnected if the conversation turned toward any kind
of politics, and my family's phones became unreachable whenever
there were protests, so it was not a surprise that Yula's phone was
being monitored. Ridiculous, but not a surprise.

Yula had called home about half an hour before we arrived,
roughly three o'clock in the morning. Someone must have been up
in the middle of the night monitoring his phone and heard that I had
arrived and would be at his house. The police showed up around
eight in the morning, less than five hours after I arrived. It must have
been one of their first duties of the day.

We did not stay around Yula's house to see if the police came back;
we were too eager to go to my parents' village. Yula borrowed a car
and drove us the forty-five minutes or so to the village. So many
memories came back to me during the ride. Not much had changed
since my childhood. I saw familiar landmarks and places I'd once
traveled to on foot. This was home. It was a great feeling to be back
in my homeland.

Outside my village with my parents, daughters, cousin, and nieces.
The monastery in the far background is the one at which I first
asked about becoming a nun.

A large crowd was waiting for us at my parents' village. Of course
my parents were there, along with Nyima and Zondija, their wives
and children, uncles and aunts, cousins, their families, and a number of neighbors. Everybody was crying when they saw me come
home—not just my parents, everyone. Even the neighbors were crying, and I was too.

Naturally another big meal was waiting for us at my father's house.
The meat was fresh, and there were several kinds of sausage made
by my father, including one I consider the best food I've ever eaten. I
was proud to show Evan the fresh natural Tibetan meat. This was real
meat, a totally different experience from the packaged meat in super-
markets. Evan liked the meat and the blood sausages, but he didn't
enjoy my favorite sausage very much. I couldn't believe it. I thought
about the first time I had apple pie and wasn't that impressed either,
and guessed maybe he needed time to get used to it.

Secret policemen showed up in the village after lunch. They knocked on my father's gate and told the person who answered to send me out to their car to talk to them. They parked in a vacant and secluded place to avoid being seen. The entire questioning, all three hours of it, took place in the car. It was a very strange experience.

First they wanted to know how I got to India, where I lived while I was there, where I went to school, and what I studied there. Then they turned to their real focus, which was getting information about other people. They wanted to know everything I knew about other exiles from Amdo. It was awkward because I didn't want to give them any information, and they did not want to let me go until I gave them something. They also wanted information about the identity and residences of all my brothers. It seemed clear they were asking about my brothers to have someone to punish in case I made any trouble while I was there.

I did my best to satisfy them without actually telling them anything by making some things up. I told them things like, "There was someone from this area named Tenzin at the Tibetan Transit School, but we weren't close." Once they had a name, they asked lots of follow-up questions, such as, "How old is Tenzin?" "Where does Tenzin live now?" and "What is he doing there?" There was no Tenzin. I could say anything and these secret police would carefully write it all down.

I don't know how they didn't suspect anything was odd about my made-up information. They seemed like low-level local police who didn't really know what they were doing. Their superiors apparently were not satisfied with their efforts, since I would later be called to submit to another round of questioning by more secret policemen from two different cities.

We brought as much medicine and clothing with us to Tibet as baggage limits allowed. The medicine, unavailable in the village, was especially valuable to my family. Vitamins we had previously sent by mail had already made a big difference to my parents' health. My mother had been having trouble standing up and sitting down, and showed remarkable improvement after she started taking vitamins. We brought clothes for everyone and watches for my new sisters-in-law.

I wanted to make a good impression on the sisters-in-law. I knew they would talk about me in the village, and it would be embarrassing if they said I didn't give them anything. Most people in Tibet thought everyone in America has more money than they can spend. After my experiences being judged and looked down on by other villagers as a child, I didn't want to be criticized anymore. I wanted people to see me as successful in life; I wanted to show them they were wrong about me.

More then coming from America or bringing nice things with me, the fact I'd seen the Dalai Lama did change the way I was viewed in the village. Only a couple other people from the village had ever seen the Dalai Lama; the widow I met in Kathmandu and one man. To the other villagers, that was the most amazing experience possible and made me something of an amazing person to them.

Evan's parents had bought quality shoes for us to bring for my parents along with a special letter from them to my parents about their happiness to have me in their life. The gifts from Evan's parents meant a lot to my mother and father. My mother cried a little as she tried the shoes on. My father was very proud of his and wore them every day. When he first tried the shoes on, he walked around very slowly to get the most out of the experience. My mother told him he should save them for special occasions, to which he replied, "I'm getting old and don't know how much longer I'll live. I better wear the shoes now to make sure I can use them."

I had to translate the letter from Evan's parents into Tibetan for my family. Tibetans don't usually promote themselves, and this letter was full of nice things about me, so it was a little embarrassing to read it in front of my family. My mother and father were very moved by Evan's parents' thoughtfulness. My father placed the letter in a special corner of the house alongside our religious images.

Our thirty–day visit in Tibet passed very quickly. There were frequent visitors to my father's house to see me, and we needed to visit my sister and Dukher in different villages. For my mother, it was an unthinkably short time. She asked how much longer we would be there almost every day. Every time she heard the answer, she looked surprised and disappointed. She'd say it was too sad for her to think about me leaving again.

Visiting in Tibet is a lot different than visiting in America. It's much more relaxed. The host is not expected to entertain visitors and show them around interesting sights. People can go out on their own and come back whenever they feel like it. If people get tired during an extended meal with friends and family, they can slide back and lie down for a nap. As long as a person can handle the food and conversation, it's easy and comfortable to stay with Tibetans for any amount of time.

Because I was visiting for the first time in so many years, and bringing my husband and children with me, my family had made certain special preparations for our visit. We stayed at my father's house for most of the trip, and they'd cleaned up everything before we came. They put away items usually left lying around, like extra clothes and kitchen utensils, anywhere they could find room. I found out about the cleaning after noticing family members searching for their belongings. In the rush to clean up, they hadn't remembered where they put everything.

I was initially worried about how Evan and the girls would respond to the absence of showers or bathrooms. I was happy to find Evan actually kind of liked the outdoor bathroom. My father's house had a stand of trees in the back surrounded by a mud wall. It was a nice peaceful atmosphere with an incredible view of the mountains. No one likes hanging around in the bathroom, but spending time in the trees looking out at the mountains is very pleasant. For occasional showers we used buckets of water like we did in India. My father took Evan to bathe down in the river one time, where there was a wonderful view of the local monastery.

Reaction to Evan and the kids was restrained in the village. Curious villagers glanced discretely from a distance or asked to shake Evan's hand. The city dwellers in Guinan were much more direct. In Guinan, we were followed everywhere by stares, pointing fingers, and a chorus of "Miku, Miku." Miku is the Chinese word for America; used by locals to identify any white person. It was often embarrassing and frustrating to be the center of attention while managing two small children. The handful of white people who had previously passed through Guinan had famously responded to the attention by acting up for the crowd. They made faces and danced around. With no other experience with white people, locals told me they thought it was normal for white people to act that way, and they wondered why my husband didn't do those things.

A couple of weeks after we arrived in the village, Yula received a phone call from the plainclothes police based in Gonghe, a large city four hours away. He was told that I needed to appear in Gonghe the next day for questioning. I asked Yula to call them back to explain that my kids and husband were sick so I wasn't able to come see them. My family wasn't sure that was smart for me to say. They thought I definitely had to go and do whatever the secret police asked.

People living in Tibet are very afraid of the government. Government authorities can do anything they want, and there is nowhere to complain, nobody to help, and nothing to do about it. Following the protests in Lhasa over the 2008 Beijing Olympics, a cousin's son was one of the victims of a sweep of suspected protestors. It's possible he did protest, but so what? In other countries, people protest all the time.

Police grabbed my cousin's son, threw him in a car, and took him away. He was never formally charged with any crimes, did not receive a trial, and no explanation was given to his family about what was happening or when he would get out. The family didn't know if he were dead or alive. His family even thought it might be good if he were dead because death is better than torture. They had recently heard about a geshe caught near the border whose bones had all been broken and was killed when the police were done torturing him. There's nothing a family can do about a situation like that except go home, pray, and cry.

My cousin's son was released six months after he disappeared. He came out a shell of the person he used to be. While in jail, he had been kept in a dark room where the police repeatedly questioned him about the identities of other people at the protest, to which he only answered that he wasn't there and didn't know who was. He had been tortured and was nearly dead from the brutality when he got out. When he left the jail, he saw sunlight for the first time since his capture, and he was amazed at the sight of the green grass outside. He was only seventeen years old.

My cousin, his father, was detained next. The police said, "We know what your son did," and threatened to put his son back in jail unless my cousin cooperated with them. They told him he had to go to India to spy on the government in exile and refugee community if he wanted to keep his son from getting arrested again. My cousin told the police he would do it, then took the entire family over the mountains into India to escape the police. They can never come home.

Zondija also had a bad experience with the Chinese police. When he was around twenty years old, he got in an argument with one of our neighbors, a longtime enemy of my father. This neighbor was a very difficult person to get along with. He was known in the village and surrounding area as Abbada, meaning "father of trouble." Abbada said many unpleasant things to Zondija until Zondija had heard enough of it and punched him. With one punch, Zondija broke two of the man's ribs. A few days later, the police showed up.

My family only found out that Zondija was with the police because someone from the village had seen the police take him. My mother went straight to Guinan to find out what was going on. She had a very hard time getting information from the police. For three days she went to the station, and every day they kicked her out when she tried to ask about Zondija. After three days, my mother found someone she knew with some connection with the police. This person was able to find out that Zondija was being held in Guinan but couldn't get any information about what was happening to him or when he would be let out. This was Zondija's first trip to the city.

Abbada had three sons working in the Chinese government, so he had influence to punish Zondija. Zondija was held for one week in the Guinan jail, and my family had to pay for all of Abbada's medical bills. Many of the bills sent to my family were unrelated to the broken ribs. Abbada could have any work done at the hospital for a long time after the incident, and the bill was always sent to my family. It looked like he was going to the hospital frequently just to make trouble.

Zondija was beaten very badly while in jail. The police station had a selection of implements for beating and shocking people hanging on the wall. A police officer would beat him with one of the implements for a long time, then switch to something else when he grew tired of using the first one. If the police officer's arm got tired from hitting Zondija, he could use other implements to shock him instead. The police paused between beatings to ponder their selection of implements. It was as if the clubs and shock devices were toys to them. By the time Zondija was released, his body was covered almost entirely in bruises. Zondija didn't want to talk about his experience; my family heard about what happened from other men who had been in jail at the same time, all of whom were forced to watch whenever someone was being beaten. The other men from the jail spoke very respectfully of Zondija as that guy from Maktangcun who never made a sound of protest or pain no matter how badly he was beaten.

Knowing what the Chinese police were capable of, my family thought it was risky for me not to comply with the order to appear for questioning in Gonghe. For me, unless the police were threatening to punish other members of my family, I wasn't intimidated by them anymore. I had the protection of American citizenship. Unlike my family members, I had a place to complain if I were harassed. If I were taken to jail without cause, Evan could bring the situation to the attention of the American embassy.

After hearing the excuse that my family was sick, the police waited a short time, then called Yula again. This time I told Yula to let them know very clearly I wasn't coming. I did not want to travel four hours away to talk to them, especially with small children. I'd already told the police in the car everything I was going to say. In any case, I didn't want to talk to them; they wanted to talk to me. If they wanted to talk to me, they could come to my door and talk.

The Chinese police could not force me to go for questioning in Gonghe and backed off a little, saying I could be questioned in Guinan instead. I agreed to that. I really didn't want to talk to them at all, but I was concerned that there might be trouble if I totally refused to meet with the secret police.

Yula went to talk with the local police before I met with my secret police interrogators. The local police were unhappy about the secret police coming to town. "What the hell do they want?" the local police chief said. The local police had me come in to have my picture taken and sign documents relating to my arrival and departure from China. It was obvious that the local police did not trust the secret police. I appreciate that they were trying to help protect me in case the secret police caused any problems.

I met one of the secret policemen in a plaza in front of the local police station. He wasn't happy to see me coming out of the police station. "You made a mistake where to go, right?" he said. It was more of a statement than a question. My husband and kids were with me, another thing he wasn't happy about. He brought us all to the best hotel in Guinan—run by the government of course.

There were a total of four men at the hotel to question me. Two were from Gonghe, and two were from the regional office based in Xining. Two men drove four hours and the other two drove six or seven hours just to question me. That was ridiculous. I wasn't doing anything illegal or crazy. I guess all the attention was flattering in a way though; I'm a very ordinary person. I'm not a lama, I don't have any information about the Tibetan government, and I'm not part of any Free Tibet organization, yet these police were making a very big deal out of my visit.

All the men were smoking when my family and I came in the room. In China, people can smoke anywhere: restaurants, buses, wherever. I told them I didn't want them smoking in front of my daughters. I said if they were going to smoke, I wanted to leave. All four of them quickly put out their cigarettes. I couldn't have done that if I had been a Chinese citizen.

The police put my husband and kids in another room down the hall while they questioned me for five continuous hours. To the frustration of the police, Evan and the girls checked in periodically to see how we were doing. I could tell the police didn't want any Western observers; they told me, "You don't need to talk about this with your husband, right?" As before, it was statement, not a question.

It was a very nice hotel for the area, and both pairs of police frequently mentioned how much better the hotels were in the larger cities they were from. They repeatedly offered to take my family and me anywhere we wanted. Each pair separately offered to drive us around their cities, show us the sights, and pay for everything.

Because my husband was visiting for the first time, they insisted we needed to be sure to stay in nice places and eat good food during our stay in China. They offered American food too if my husband wanted it. Maybe that tactic works with some people. Maybe some people come off their farms and are wowed by the luxuries the police can offer them. For me, there was no appeal at all. I didn't come all this way to have the police take me out to dinner; I was there to see my family. I only wanted them to finish up so I could leave and go back to my family again.

The meeting started with a hostile tone. "Don't think you can do whatever you want because you are from America. While you are here, you have to follow the rules here," an unpleasant man from the regional office said. I told him I wasn't there for trouble, just to see my family. They asked the same questions I'd been asked in the car my first day back in the village. These police didn't let me off with evasive answers. They said I had to give them at least ten names of people I had specific information on.

The police already had an extensive collection of information about all the refugees from the local area living abroad. One of the regional police brought up names of some of these other people and information about them. He'd say, "What about So-and-So, are you telling me you don't know anything about him?" He claimed plenty of other people had given information about me, so there was nothing wrong if I gave information about them too. My only answer was that if they already knew all this, they didn't need me. In response to a question concerning a Tibetan man working for Radio Free Asia, I pointed to the pushy man from the regional office and said, "I don't know, but he does—you should ask him."

It seemed to me most of the questions were pointless. I seriously didn't know anything of value to them, even if I had been willing to cooperate. It's hard to imagine what they do with information they collect about other simple refugees like me. They said they had information about me, okay, so what about me? I'm mostly focused on my family, which has zero to do with them. Some of the questions were about Evan and his family, and again, I can't see how that could be helpful to the Chinese government in any way.

The two policemen from Gonghe and the two from Xining didn't appear to be coordinated. They took breaks separately, and while one pair was out of the room, the other two would make an appeal for me to come see just them later. Both pairs of police suggested I could trust them and not necessarily the other two. The ones from Gonghe in particular pushed the idea that they didn't like the men from Xining any more than I did. I got the impression that the police from Gonghe were under some pressure not to be outdone by the regional police, but if nobody got information, they were okay.

This session lasted a solid five hours. In total, including the session in the car, it added up to eight hours of interrogation. The police took breaks during these five hours; I did not. There were four men in the room surrounding me, alone with them. I'm curious how often they succeed at getting information out of people. I certainly would have felt more pressure to comply if I weren't an American citizen; it's possible some people get nervous and give in.

Part of the reason the interrogation took so long was that the police wrote everything down by hand. They not only wrote every-thing by hand, they frequently had to rewrite sections by hand if they made any errors. They were very concerned about making errors. The reports were evidently going to be viewed by highly critical superiors. I asked why they didn't use computers to save time, knowing full well that they either didn't have computers or couldn't use them. The answer they gave me was confusing, something about how writing by hand was a way of keeping their traditions.

My mother was extremely worried the entire time I was with the police. She went to the village chorten to walk around it praying for my safety until she received word I was done. I feel sorry that she had to experience that. She had already seen a lot in her life; she was almost certainly imagining all the very real dangers I could face if the police wanted to make trouble for me.

My plan had been to return to my parents' village as soon as the questioning was over, but the session went too long. We stayed with Yula for the night, and heavy rains brought mudslides onto the roads while we slept. It took several days to clear the roads again. When we got back, Kobi was out with his goats, and my father enlisted Evan to help him with a couple of projects. One of the projects was to repair a large cutting board. This cutting board had a special purpose: It was for the village to use during the prayers after my father died. My father was eager to complete it so he would be ready for death. His coffin, more of a simple box in Tibet, was already built and waiting for him.

My father, like most older Tibetans, treated the prospect of death as a fact of old age he needed to be prepared for. Death is not necessarily frightening or depressing in the view of aging Tibetans like my father. Most elders cheerfully stepped aside whenever Evan or I took group photographs in Tibet because they thought we would have to burn the photo when they died. If I argued that they weren't very old and would most likely be around a long time, the response was usually a laugh and protest that they were actually very old and were not expecting to live much longer.

Tibetans expect to be reborn again, typically within their own family. New parents often look for birthmarks on their children corresponding to bedsores from deceased family members. When a reincarnation is identified, relatives of the deceased person have a special relationship with the new baby.

I suspect that Tenny may be the reincarnation of someone from my village. I had recurring dreams about this person during my pregnancy. It was the father of a girl in the village I had advised to become a nun. Her father had always liked me as a young child, but he later considered me responsible for his daughter's decision to become a nun and never forgave me for it. After I started having these dreams, I asked my family members how the father was doing and found out that he had died. I can't be sure, and I have my own doubts, but I think it's possible his mental attachment concerning me influenced his rebirth.

32. White Stones

WHITE STONES dominated my final days in Tibet. We all gathered them for Zondija, who had a tall order to fill. Deeply affected by Prri's death, Zondija lacked focus, and his life was troubled. He remained distant from the family, holding on to his private sadness. His wife did not appreciate his choice of consolation, which was drinking and gambling. A lama sought out by my family had offered to perform a special blessing to bring Zondija peace and stability, with one condition—first, Zondija had to collect one hundred thousand white stones for the ceremony.

He'd started collecting the stones years before I came home and given up at least once, more likely two or three times. The fruit of his abandoned efforts were piled on his porch, the count forgotten until my visit became the occasion for a big push by the whole family to finish the task. We'd ride to the riverbed on a tractor-pulled cart, as many of us as could fit, carrying burlap sacks to collect our stones in. The stones had to be just right: pure white, smooth, and round, with no cracks or chips. They also couldn't be very big, definitely smaller than a thumb, only because there were so many to carry and store.

Initially, collecting white stones was an aggravating task. My mind struggled to concentrate on selecting the small white stones out of an expanse of many colored stones before us, and progress was mad-deningly slow. The small satisfaction of finding each suitable stone was immediately crushed by the thought of how many were left to go. After the initial minutes, however, the experience would shift, gradually becoming peaceful and liberating. I became fully absorbed in the experience, and concentration became effortless. All I could see was the white stones.

The feeling of being out with my family collecting those stones for Zondija meant a lot to me. Zondija wasn't on his own. He didn't need to beg for help or offer anything in return, and there was no need for any thank you's. It was something my family did for him just because we're family. The lama who gave Zondija this task knew what he was doing. The meditative experience of gathering the stones and the connection of family working together to help one member already went a long way toward bringing peace and stability before the lama even performed his ceremony.

As the end of our thirty days in Tibet neared, I was having sec-ond thoughts about leaving. I'd dreamed about seeing my family again for so many years; it didn't seem possible that I could walk away from them a second time after such a short visit. Going home again had only reminded me of everything I had there, everything I missed.

My family members encouraged me to consider staying. Kobi offered to give Evan and me half of everything he owned if we stayed in Tibet. The Amdo dialect doesn't have a word for sorry, but I think that was his way of apologizing for the time he and my father beat me. Obviously, my mother didn't want us to leave. It was difficult to decide either way whether to go back to America or stay in Tibet and take my chances with getting approved as a resident. On the one hand, I had a life in America to think about. On the other, how could I say goodbye to my Tibetan family, not knowing if I would get another chance to see them again?

I feel grateful to my parents for taking care of me as a child. Now that they are getting old, it hurts me that I'm not able to show my appreciation by caring for them now. I've carried my regrets about leaving them with me for many years, feeling helpless in my inability to do much about it. Before my return, I'd dreamed about having the chance to do simple things like preparing a meal for my mother, washing my father's clothes, or cleaning up for them. Being there with them in Tibet, I didn't want to leave. If I only had myself to think about, I would not have come back to America.

Reminding myself that I am the mother of two children who I needed to put ahead of my own desires, I went through with all the preparations to leave. I said goodbye to my parents in Guinan. They came as far as the bus stop to see us off. My sister and one of Yula's sons came as far as the airport in Xining. At the airport, as I faced my final chance to turn back before fully committing myself to returning to America, my mind was very torn. Once I went through that security gate, I would be truly leaving Tibet and my family behind. We would continue into the airport and pass from their view, and then the last of my family members would go home without me.

I went through the security gate. Although Evan has said he would rather live with me happy in Tibet than miserable in America, I love him too much to reverse our fates. I would have to give up my American citizenship to live in Tibet again, leaving us without an escape if Evan found he was unhappy there, or permanently torn apart in the likely event China refused to grant Evan permanent residence after I became a Chinese citizen.

Now that I'm back in America, I've earned my driver's license, and I have a job working in a dining hall at Bowdoin College. This new job is much better than the daycare. I'm treated well, I get along with my coworkers, and I don't mind the work. I'm more independent than I used to be, and I still have the support of a good family. Evan is a good husband and the best father I've ever seen. His parents have given me all of their love, making me feel like they are my own second parents.

It's not a fairytale ending for me, but it's enough for me to hold on to and keep me standing. After this many years in America, I can see that I am not going to stop missing my family and homeland. A piece of my heart will always be in Tibet. I cannot give up my hope that one day the situation in Tibet will change. For as long as Tibet is occupied, I will always be here waiting for the day I can go home again with my family, waiting for freedom.

To Learn More

View extra content and follow Kunsang Dolma's story as it continues to unfold on her blog: **100kwhitestones.wordpress.com**.

News

Keep abreast of news about Tibet, Tibetans in exile, and the Tibetan struggle for self-determination in their homeland at the following websites:

- Central Tibetan Administration (Tibetan Government in Exile): www.tibet.net
- The International Campaign for Tibet: www.savetibet.org
- Voice of America–Tibetan (in English): voatibetanenglish.com

Aid

Assistance to those truly in need is never forgotten. If you would like to contribute to a Tibetan charity or support the Tibetan people, consider the following organizations.

treesfortibet.blogspot.com
Trees for Tibet is a grassroots project organized by villagers in eastern Tibet to battle desertification and prevent destruction of the grasslands that support their nomadic culture.

tcv.org.in
The Tibetan Children's Village (TCV) is an integrated educational community where destitute Tibetan children living in exile can gain access to a full K–12 education. TCV serves over sixteen thousand children at branches in India.

tnp.org
The Tibetan Nuns Project provides education and humanitarian aid to refugee nuns and works to improve the status of ordained women in general. Based in Dharamsala, India, the Project provides facilities and programs for more than 700 Tibetan women.

For an alphabetical listing of a wide array of Tibet support groups, please consult Tibet Online at tibet.org/Resources/TSG/Groups.

Further Reading

To learn more about Tibetan history, religion, and culture, we recommend the following books.

TIBETAN HISTORY

Tibet: A History / Sam Van Schaik. New Haven: Yale University Press, 2011.
The Story of Tibet: Conversations with the Dalai Lama / Thomas Laird. New York: Grove Press, 2007.
The Dragon in the Land of Snows: A History of Modern Tibet Since 1947 / Tsering Shakya. New York: Penguin, 1999.

BUDDHISM

The Compassionate Life / The Dalai Lama. Boston: Wisdom Publications, 2003.

Tibetan Buddhism from the Ground Up / B. Alan Wallace. Boston: Wisdom
  Publications, 1994.

*The Words of My Perfect Teacher: A Complete Translation of a Classic Introduction
  to Tibetan Buddhism* / Patrul Rinpoche. Translated by the Padmakara
  Translation Group. New Haven CT: Yale University Press, 2010.

An End to Suffering: The Buddha in the World / Pankaj Mishra. New York:
  Picador, 2004.

MEMOIR

Freedom in Exile: The Autobiography of the Dalai Lama / The Dalai Lama.
  New York: Harper Collins, 1990.

The Voice that Remembers: A Tibetan Woman's Inspiring Story of Survival /
  Ama Adhe and Joy Blakeslee. Boston: Wisdom Publications, 1997.

Cave in the Snow: Tenzin Palmo's Quest for Enlightenment / Vicki Mackenzie.
  New York: Bloomsbury, 1998.

About Wisdom Publications

Wisdom Publications is dedicated to offering works relating to and inspired by Buddhist traditions.

To learn more about us or to explore our other books, please visit our website at www.wisdompubs.org.

You can subscribe to our e-newsletter or request our print catalog online, or by writing to:

Wisdom Publications
199 Elm Street
Somerville, Massachusetts 02144 USA

You can also contact us at 617-776-7416, or info@wisdompubs.org.

Wisdom is a nonprofit, charitable 501(c)(3) organization, and donations in support of our mission are tax deductible.

Wisdom Publications is affiliated with the Foundation for the Preservation of the Mahayana Tradition (FPMT).